SARA L. WESTON

The Secrets of Bj581: Birka Female Warrior

This book was professionally typeset on Reedsy.
Find out more at reedsy.com

Contents

Preface

Through research and analysis, this book uncovers the controversies that have surrounded the Birka Warrior since her discovery. It examines the debates among scholars regarding her gender, social status, and role in Viking society. By examining the various theories and interpretations, readers gain a comprehensive understanding of the complexities surrounding this enigmatic figure.

Understanding the significance of the Birka Warrior as a female ruler is crucial in recognizing the existence of gender fluidity throughout history. This book explores the implications of her discovery on our understanding of gender roles in ancient societies. It challenges preconceived notions and encourages readers to reconsider the roles and contributions of women in the past. By unraveling the mysteries of the Birka Warrior, this book offers a fresh perspective on the rich and diverse history of female leadership.

I

Part One

Book Overview
The "Birka Warrior: Unveiling the Mysteries of the Female Ruler" is a captivating exploration of the remarkable discovery of a female warrior buried in Birka, Sweden. This book delves into the historical context, archaeological evidence, and cultural significance surrounding this extraordinary find. By shedding light on the life and identity of the Birka Warrior, it challenges traditional notions of gender roles and highlights the existence of powerful women in ancient societies.

II

Part Two

Uncovering The Grave

1

Chapter 1

Introduction

1.1 The Discovery of the Birka Warrior

The Birka Warrior, also known as the Birka female Viking warrior or the Viking woman warrior, refers to the archaeological discovery of a burial site in Birka, Sweden, that challenges traditional gender roles and assumptions in Viking society. The Birka Warrior was found in the late 19th century during excavations led by Swedish archaeologist Hjalmar Stolpe. The burial site, designated as grave Bj 581, contained a wealth of artifacts and weapons typically associated with male warriors, leading to the initial assumption that the individual buried there was a man.

However, in recent years, the remains were reevaluated using modern scientific techniques, including DNA analysis and osteological examinations. These investigations revealed that the Birka Warrior was, in fact, a woman. This groundbreaking discovery has sparked significant controversy and debate within the archaeological and historical communities.

The controversies surrounding the Birka Warrior primarily revolve around the traditional gender roles and expectations in Viking society. The prevailing view of Vikings as exclusively male warriors and raiders has been challenged by this discovery. It forces us to reconsider the roles and contributions of women in Viking society and the extent to which they participated in warfare and held positions of power.

Understanding that the Birka Warrior was a female is crucial because it challenges the long-held assumption that Viking warriors were exclusively male. It highlights the complexity and diversity of gender roles in the Viking Age and provides evidence of women engaging in traditionally male-dominated activities, such as warfare. This discovery also sheds light on the existence of female rulers and leaders in Viking society, which was previously overlooked or dismissed.

The significance of the Birka Warrior's gender extends beyond the Viking Age. It serves as a reminder that gender fluidity and non-binary identities have existed throughout history. The discovery challenges the notion that gender roles and expectations are fixed and unchanging. It demonstrates that societies have historically accommodated and recognized individuals who do not conform to traditional gender norms.

By acknowledging the existence of the Birka Warrior and other similar historical figures, we can challenge the binary understanding of gender and promote a more inclusive and nuanced understanding of human identity. It encourages us to question the rigid gender constructs that persist in modern society and recognize the fluidity of gender expression and identity.

The Birka Warrior's discovery also highlights the importance of interdisciplinary research and the integration of scientific methods in archaeological investigations. The use of DNA analysis and osteological examinations allowed researchers to uncover the true identity of the Birka Warrior, challenging previous assumptions based solely on material culture. This interdisciplinary approach has the potential to reshape our understanding of the past and uncover hidden narratives that have been overlooked or marginalized.

In conclusion, the discovery of the Birka Warrior challenges traditional gender roles and assumptions in Viking society. It highlights the existence of female warriors and leaders, providing evidence of gender fluidity and non-binary identities in the past. Understanding the significance of the Birka Warrior's gender expands our knowledge of Viking society and encourages us to reevaluate gender norms and stereotypes in both historical and contemporary contexts

1.2 Controversies Surrounding the Birka Warrior

The discovery of the Birka Warrior, a female Viking warrior buried with weapons and other traditionally male-associated grave goods, has sparked significant controversy and debate among archaeologists, historians, and scholars. Unearthed in the late 19th century at the Viking Age trading center of Birka in Sweden, the burial site has challenged long-held assumptions about gender roles in Viking society and has raised important questions about the fluidity of gender identity throughout history.

One of the main controversies surrounding the Birka Warrior revolves around the initial assumption that the individual buried with weapons and armor must have been male. For many years, the prevailing belief was that Viking warriors were exclusively male, and any evidence suggesting otherwise was often dismissed or overlooked. The discovery of the Birka Warrior challenged this assumption and forced a reevaluation of gender norms in Viking society.

Critics of the interpretation that the Birka Warrior was a female have argued that the presence of weapons and armor in the grave does not necessarily indicate a warrior status. They suggest that the individual may have been buried with these items as symbols of prestige or as offerings to the deceased. Additionally, some skeptics have questioned the accuracy of the archaeological findings, suggesting that the burial may have been misinterpreted or that the grave goods were incorrectly associated with the individual.

Another controversy surrounding the Birka Warrior is the resistance to accepting the possibility of female warriors in Viking society. Traditional historical accounts and sagas often depict male warriors, leading some to argue that the presence of a female warrior challenges the authenticity of these narratives. However, it is important to recognize that historical accounts are often biased and incomplete, and the absence of explicit references to female warriors does not necessarily mean they did not exist.

Understanding that the Birka Warrior was a female is crucial for several reasons. Firstly, it challenges the long-held assumption that Viking warriors were exclusively male. This discovery highlights the need to reevaluate gender roles in the Viking Age and recognize that women may have played a more active and diverse role in warfare and leadership than previously acknowledged.

Furthermore, the Birka Warrior's gender challenges the notion that gender fluidity is a modern concept. The burial site provides evidence that individuals in the Viking Age may have had more fluid gender identities and expressions than previously assumed. The presence of a female warrior suggests that gender roles were not fixed and that individuals could transcend societal expectations and engage in activities traditionally associated with the opposite gender.

By acknowledging the existence of the Birka Warrior and other similar archaeological findings, we gain a deeper understanding of the complexity of gender identity throughout history. It challenges the notion that gender is a binary construct and highlights the existence of diverse gender expressions and roles in different cultures and time periods.

The controversies surrounding the Birka Warrior serve as a reminder of the limitations of our knowledge and the biases that can influence our interpretations of the past. It emphasizes the importance of approaching archaeological and historical evidence with an open mind and a willingness to challenge established narratives.

In conclusion, the discovery of the Birka Warrior has sparked significant controversies and debates within the academic community. The burial site challenges long-held assumptions about gender roles in Viking society and highlights the fluidity of gender identity throughout history. Understanding the significance of the Birka Warrior as a female warrior is crucial for reevaluating gender norms in the Viking Age and recognizing the existence of diverse gender expressions and roles. This discovery serves as a reminder of the limitations of our knowledge and the importance of questioning established narratives in order to gain a more comprehensive understanding of the past.

1.3 The Significance of the Birka Warrior's Gender

The Birka Warrior, also known as the Birka female Viking warrior or the Viking woman warrior, refers to the discovery of a burial site in Birka, Sweden, that contained the remains of a high-status individual buried with weapons and other artifacts traditionally associated with male warriors. The discovery of this burial site in the late 19th century sparked significant controversy and debate among archaeologists and historians.

The Birka Warrior was found in the mid-1880s by Swedish archaeologist Hjalmar Stolpe during excavations at the Viking Age trading center of Birka. The burial site, known as grave Bj 581, contained the remains of a warrior accompanied by a variety of grave goods, including a sword, spear, shield, and two horses. These artifacts, along with the presence of gaming pieces and a gaming board, suggested a high-status individual of great importance.

The controversies surrounding the Birka Warrior primarily revolve around the gender of the individual buried in grave Bj 581. Initially, it was assumed that the burial belonged to a male warrior due to the presence of weapons and the traditional association of such artifacts with male burials. However, in recent years, a reevaluation of the burial and its context has led to the conclusion that the Birka Warrior was, in fact, a female.

The significance of the Birka Warrior's gender lies in challenging long-held assumptions about gender roles and expectations in Viking society. The prevailing belief that Viking warriors were exclusively male has been called into question by this discovery. It forces us to reconsider the roles and contributions of women in Viking society and challenges the notion that women were solely confined to domestic and nurturing roles.

Understanding that the Birka Warrior was a female warrior sheds light on the existence of gender fluidity in the Viking Age and throughout history. It demonstrates that gender roles were not fixed or rigid, but rather varied and flexible. The Birka Warrior's burial challenges the binary understanding of gender and highlights the fluidity of gender identity and expression in Viking culture.

The presence of a female warrior in the Birka burial site suggests that women in Viking society had the opportunity to participate in warfare and hold positions of power and authority. It challenges the notion that women were passive participants in Viking society and highlights their agency and autonomy. The Birka Warrior's gender challenges the traditional narrative of male dominance in Viking society and provides evidence of a more complex and diverse social structure.

The discovery of the Birka Warrior's gender also has broader implications for our understanding of gender fluidity through-out history. It serves as a reminder that gender identities and ex-pressions have existed in various forms across different cultures and time periods. The Birka Warrior's burial challenges the notion that gender fluidity is a modern concept and highlights its presence in ancient societies.

By acknowledging the existence of gender fluidity in the past, we can challenge contemporary assumptions and stereotypes about gender. It encourages us to question the binary un-derstanding of gender and recognize the diversity of human experiences and identities. The Birka Warrior's burial serves as a powerful reminder that gender is not fixed or determined solely by biological sex, but rather a complex interplay of social, cultural, and individual factors.

In conclusion, the significance of the Birka Warrior's gender lies in challenging long-held assumptions about gender roles in Viking society and shedding light on the existence of gender fluidity throughout history. The discovery of a female warrior buried with weapons and high-status grave goods challenges traditional narratives of male dominance in Viking society and highlights the agency and autonomy of women. Understanding the Birka Warrior's gender expands our understanding of gender fluidity and encourages us to question binary understandings of gender in both the past and present.

1.4 Gender Fluidity Throughout History

Throughout history, the concept of gender has been fluid and has varied across different cultures and time periods. The discovery of the Birka Warrior, a female Viking warrior buried with weapons and armor traditionally associated with men, challenges the traditional understanding of gender roles in Viking society. This discovery has sparked controversies and raised important questions about the role of gender fluidity in history.

The Birka Warrior, also known as the Bj 581 grave, was discovered in the late 19th century in Birka, an ancient Viking trading center located in present-day Sweden. The grave contained the remains of a high-status individual buried with a variety of weapons, including a sword, spear, and shield, as well as gaming pieces and a horse. The presence of these items initially led archaeologists to assume that the individual was a male warrior.

However, in recent years, a reevaluation of the grave and its contents has challenged this assumption. Through the use of modern scientific techniques, including DNA analysis, it was determined that the Birka Warrior was, in fact, a woman. This revelation has ignited debates and controversies within the archaeological community, as it challenges long-held beliefs about gender roles in Viking society.

Understanding that the Birka Warrior was a female is significant for several reasons. Firstly, it challenges the notion that women in Viking society were solely confined to domestic roles. The presence of weapons and armor in the grave suggests that women had the ability to participate in warfare and hold positions of power and authority. This challenges the traditional narrative that Viking women were passive and subservient.

Secondly, the discovery of the Birka Warrior highlights the existence of gender fluidity in Viking society. Gender fluidity refers to the idea that gender is not fixed and can change or be expressed in various ways. In Viking culture, gender roles were not as rigidly defined as in some other societies. There is evidence to suggest that Viking society recognized and accepted individuals who did not conform to traditional gender norms.

Historical accounts and sagas mention the existence of female warriors, known as shieldmaidens, who fought alongside men in battle. These shieldmaidens were often depicted as strong and skilled fighters, challenging the notion that warfare was exclusively a male domain. The presence of the Birka Warrior adds further weight to the existence of these female warriors and suggests that they held positions of power and authority within Viking society.

The concept of gender fluidity is not unique to Viking culture. Throughout history, many societies have recognized and accepted individuals who did not conform to traditional gender norms. In ancient Rome, for example, there were individuals known as eunuchs who occupied a unique gender category. In

Native American cultures, there were individuals known as Two-Spirit who embodied both masculine and feminine qualities.

Understanding the existence of gender fluidity throughout history is important for several reasons. Firstly, it challenges the notion that gender is a fixed and binary concept. It highlights the diversity of human experiences and identities, and the fact that gender is a social construct that can vary across different cultures and time periods.

Secondly, recognizing the existence of gender fluidity in history helps to challenge and dismantle harmful stereotypes and prejudices. It promotes inclusivity and acceptance of individuals who do not conform to traditional gender norms. By acknowledging the historical presence of gender fluidity, we can work towards creating a more inclusive and equitable society today.

In conclusion, the discovery of the Birka Warrior and the recognition of her as a female Viking warrior challenges traditional notions of gender roles in Viking society. It highlights the existence of gender fluidity throughout history and the acceptance of individuals who did not conform to traditional gender norms. Understanding and acknowledging the historical presence of gender fluidity is important for promoting inclusivity and acceptance in modern society.

2

Chapter 2

The Viking Age and Birka

2.1 Overview of the Viking Age

The Viking Age, spanning from the late 8th century to the early 11th century, was a significant period in European history characterized by Norse exploration, trade, and raiding activities. This era witnessed the expansion of Scandinavian seafarers, known as Vikings, who ventured far from their homelands in present-day Norway, Sweden, and Denmark. The Viking Age was a time of great cultural, social, and political change, and it played a crucial role in shaping the history of Europe.

During this period, the Vikings established trade routes, explored new lands, and engaged in both peaceful and hostile interactions with various cultures. They were skilled navigators and shipbuilders, using their longships to travel across vast distances, including the North Atlantic, the Baltic Sea, and even as far as the Mediterranean. The Vikings' seafaring abilities allowed them to establish trade networks, leading to the exchange of goods, ideas, and technologies with other societies.

One of the most significant Viking trading centers was Birka, located on the island of Björkö in Lake Mälaren, Sweden. Birka served as a vital hub for commerce, connecting the Baltic Sea region with the wider Viking world. It was a bustling cosmopolitan town, attracting merchants, craftsmen, and travelers from various parts of Europe and beyond. The strategic location of Birka made it an ideal center for trade, as it provided access to both the Baltic Sea and the inland waterways.

Archaeological excavations at Birka have provided valuable insights into Viking society and culture. The discoveries made at this site have shed light on various aspects of Viking life, including their social structure, economic activities, and religious beliefs. The most remarkable find at Birka was the burial site of a warrior, commonly referred to as the "Birka Warrior."

The Birka Warrior's grave was discovered in the late 19th century by Swedish archaeologist Hjalmar Stolpe. The burial, dating back to the 10th century, contained a wealth of grave goods and artifacts, including weapons, armor, personal items, and jewelry. Initially, it was assumed that the Birka Warrior was a male due to the presence of these traditionally masculine items. However, subsequent analysis and reevaluation of the burial revealed that the individual was, in fact, a female.

This revelation sparked significant controversies and debates among scholars and archaeologists. The idea of a female warrior challenged long-held assumptions about gender roles in Viking society. It forced a reevaluation of the prevailing narrative that Vikings were predominantly male warriors, while women played passive and domestic roles. The discovery of the Birka Warrior highlighted the complexity and fluidity of gender identities in the Viking Age.

Understanding that the Birka Warrior was a female is crucial for several reasons. Firstly, it challenges the traditional notion that women in Viking society were confined to domestic roles. It suggests that women had the agency and capability to participate in warfare and hold positions of power and authority. This challenges the stereotypical view of Viking women as passive and submissive.

Secondly, the discovery of the Birka Warrior emphasizes the existence of gender fluidity in the Viking Age. It indicates that gender roles and expressions were not fixed or rigid, but rather varied and adaptable. The presence of a female warrior suggests that gender identity was not solely determined by biological sex but could be influenced by social, cultural, and individual factors.

This understanding of gender fluidity in the Viking Age has broader implications for our understanding of gender throughout history. It challenges the notion that gender binaries and strict gender roles are universal and timeless. Instead, it highlights the diversity and complexity of gender identities across different cultures and time periods.

The Birka Warrior's story serves as a powerful reminder that gender fluidity and non-conformity have existed for centuries. It challenges the notion that these concepts are recent social constructs or products of modern society. By recognizing the presence of female warriors and the fluidity of gender in the Viking Age, we gain a deeper understanding of the complexities of human identity and the ways in which societies have historically navigated and understood gender.

2.2 Birka

Birka, located on the island of Björkö in Lake Mälaren, Sweden, was a prominent trading center during the Viking Age. It flourished from the late 8th century to the early 10th century and played a crucial role in the economic and cultural exchange between Scandinavia and the wider world. The site's strategic location made it a hub for trade routes, attracting merchants from various regions.

Birka's significance lies not only in its economic prosperity but also in its archaeological remains, which provide valuable insights into Viking society. Excavations at Birka have unearthed a wealth of artifacts, including weapons, tools, jewelry, and burial sites. One of the most intriguing discoveries was the grave of the Birka Warrior, a burial mound that has sparked considerable controversy and fascination.

The Birka Warrior, also known as Grave Bj 581, was discovered in 1878 by Swedish archaeologist Hjalmar Stolpe. The grave contained a rich assortment of weapons, including a sword, spear, shield, and arrows, as well as gaming pieces, a comb, and other personal items. These grave goods indicated that the individual buried there held a high status within Viking society.

The controversy surrounding the Birka Warrior primarily revolves around the assumption that the grave belonged to a male warrior. For many years, the prevailing belief was that only men were buried with such elaborate weaponry. However, in recent decades, a reevaluation of gender in archaeology has challenged this assumption and opened up new possibilities.

The significance of the Birka Warrior's gender lies in the fact that it challenges traditional notions of gender roles in Viking society. The assumption that only men held positions of power and engaged in warfare has been called into question. The presence of a female warrior challenges the binary understanding of gender and highlights the fluidity of gender roles in the Viking Age.

Understanding that gender fluidity has existed for centuries is crucial in dispelling the notion that gender roles are fixed and unchanging. The Birka Warrior's existence suggests that women in Viking society had the agency to participate in traditionally male-dominated activities, such as warfare. This challenges the idea that women were solely confined to domestic roles and were passive participants in Viking society.

The Birka Warrior's burial site provides evidence of a female ruler or leader who held significant power and influence. This challenges the prevailing narrative that positions of authority were exclusively reserved for men. The presence of a female warrior suggests that women in Viking society could attain positions of leadership and command respect from their peers.

Furthermore, the Birka Warrior's existence sheds light on the complexity of gender identity in the Viking Age. It suggests that individuals may have identified and expressed their gender in ways that did not conform to traditional binary norms. This challenges the notion that gender identity is a modern construct and highlights the existence of diverse gender expressions throughout history.

The discovery of the Birka Warrior also has implications for contemporary society. It serves as a reminder that gender equality and fluidity are not recent concepts but have deep historical roots. The recognition of the Birka Warrior as a female ruler challenges societal norms and encourages a more inclusive understanding of gender.

By acknowledging the existence of powerful female leaders

in the past, the Birka Warrior's story becomes a source of inspiration for women today. It highlights the potential for women to break free from societal constraints and pursue positions of power and influence. The Birka Warrior's legacy serves as a symbol of empowerment and resilience, inspiring women to challenge gender norms and strive for equality.

In conclusion, Birka was a significant trading center during the Viking Age, and the discovery of the Birka Warrior's burial site has sparked controversy and fascination. The presence of a female warrior challenges traditional gender roles and highlights the fluidity of gender identity in the Viking Age. Understanding the Birka Warrior's story is important in recognizing the historical existence of powerful female leaders and inspiring contemporary efforts towards gender equality.

2.3 Archaeological Excavations at Birka

The archaeological excavations at Birka have played a crucial role in unraveling the mysteries surrounding the Birka Warrior. Birka, located on the island of Björkö in Lake Mälaren, Sweden, was a prominent trading center during the Viking Age. The site was first excavated in the late 19th century by Swedish archaeologist Hjalmar Stolpe, and it continues to be a significant area of study for researchers interested in Viking history and culture.

The initial discovery of the Birka Warrior took place in the late 19th century during Stolpe's excavations. The burial mound, known as Bj 581, contained the remains of a high-status individual accompanied by an array of weapons, armor, and other grave goods typically associated with male warriors. However, it was not until the 1970s that the remains were reexamined and identified as those of a female.

The identification of the Birka Warrior as a female sparked significant controversy within the archaeological community. Traditional gender roles and assumptions had long dictated that Viking warriors were exclusively male. The idea of a female warrior challenged these preconceived notions and raised questions about the role of women in Viking society. Some scholars initially dismissed the possibility of a female warrior, suggesting that the grave goods may have been misinterpreted or that the burial was a result of grave robbing and subsequent disturbance.

However, subsequent research and reevaluations of the burial have provided compelling evidence supporting the identification of the Birka Warrior as a female. The presence of weapons and armor, typically associated with male warriors, suggests that she held a high-status position within Viking society. Furthermore, isotopic analysis of the remains has indicated that she likely spent her childhood in a region outside of Birka, suggesting that she may have come from a distant land and held a position of authority.

Understanding that the Birka Warrior was a female is of utmost importance in challenging traditional gender roles and shedding light on the complexity of Viking society. It demonstrates that women in the Viking Age were not confined to domestic roles but could also participate in warfare and hold positions of power. This challenges the notion that gender roles were fixed and highlights the fluidity of gender identity in the past.

The existence of the Birka Warrior also provides evidence of gender fluidity in Viking culture. While the concept of gender fluidity may be seen as a modern phenomenon, the

Birka Warrior's burial challenges this assumption. It suggests that the acceptance and recognition of individuals who did not conform to traditional gender norms may have existed in Viking society. This challenges the notion that gender fluidity is a recent development and emphasizes that diverse gender expressions have been present throughout history.

By acknowledging the presence of a female warrior in Viking society, we gain a deeper understanding of the complexities of gender roles and identities in the past. It allows us to challenge the binary understanding of gender and recognize that societies have historically accommodated a range of gender expressions. This understanding has significant implications for contemporary discussions surrounding gender equality and LGBTQ+ rights.

The archaeological excavations at Birka have not only provided valuable insights into the life of the Birka Warrior but have also contributed to our understanding of Viking society as a whole. The discovery challenges long-held assumptions about gender roles and highlights the need for a more nuanced interpretation of historical evidence. As we continue to explore and analyze Viking-age sites, it is crucial to approach the evidence with an open mind and consider the diverse possibilities of gender expression and identity in the past.

2.4 The Birka Warrior's Burial Site

The discovery of the Birka Warrior's burial site has provided invaluable insights into the Viking Age and the role of women in Viking society. Located in the ancient trading center of Birka, on the island of Björkö in Sweden, the burial site was unearthed in the late 19th century by Swedish archaeologist Hjalmar Stolpe.

The Birka Warrior, as she came to be known, was found buried with a wealth of grave goods and artifacts typically associated with high-ranking individuals.

However, the identification of the Birka Warrior as a female has sparked significant controversy and debate among scholars and archaeologists. The prevailing assumption in the past was that Viking warriors were exclusively male, and any evidence suggesting otherwise was often dismissed or overlooked. The discovery of a female buried with weapons and armor challenged these preconceived notions and forced a reevaluation of gender roles in Viking society.

Understanding that the Birka Warrior was a female is crucial for several reasons. Firstly, it challenges the traditional narrative that women in the Viking Age were confined to domestic roles and were not involved in warfare or held positions of power. The presence of weapons and armor in her grave suggests that she was a skilled warrior, defying societal expectations and highlighting the agency and autonomy of women in Viking society.

Furthermore, the Birka Warrior's burial site provides evidence of gender fluidity in the Viking Age. While the concept of gender fluidity may be seen as a modern phenomenon, the existence of individuals who did not conform to traditional gender norms has been observed throughout history. The Birka Warrior's burial challenges the binary understanding of gender and highlights the fluidity and complexity of gender identities in the past.

By acknowledging the existence of gender fluidity in the Viking Age, we gain a deeper understanding of the diversity of human experiences and the ways in which societies have historically navigated and accepted non-binary gender identities. This challenges the notion that gender fluidity is a recent development or a product of contemporary culture. Instead, it reveals that diverse gender expressions have existed for centuries, even in societies that are often perceived as rigidly patriarchal.

The Birka Warrior's burial site also raises questions about the social and cultural context in which she lived. Her high-status burial, complete with weapons, armor, and other prestigious grave goods, suggests that she held a position of power and authority within Viking society. This challenges the assumption that women in the Viking Age were solely relegated to domestic roles and were excluded from positions of leadership.

The significance of the Birka Warrior's burial site extends beyond the Viking Age. It serves as a reminder that gender equality and the acceptance of diverse gender identities are not recent concepts, but rather have deep historical roots. By recognizing the existence of powerful female figures like the Birka Warrior, we can challenge and dismantle gender stereotypes and work towards a more inclusive and equitable society.

In conclusion, the Birka Warrior's burial site provides a fascinating glimpse into the complexities of gender roles and identities in the Viking Age. The discovery challenges traditional assumptions about women in Viking society and highlights the existence of gender fluidity throughout history. By understanding and appreciating the significance of the Birka Warrior's burial, we can gain a deeper understanding of the diverse experiences of individuals in the past and work towards a more inclusive and accepting future.

3

Chapter 3

The Birka Warrior's Grave

3.1 Description of the Grave

The grave of the Birka Warrior is a remarkable archaeological discovery that sheds light on the complexities of gender roles and identities in Viking society. Located in the ancient trading center of Birka, on the island of Björkö in present-day Sweden, the grave was unearthed in the late 19th century by Swedish archaeologist Hjalmar Stolpe. The Birka Warrior, as she came to be known, was found buried with a rich array of grave goods and artifacts, indicating her high status and importance within the community.

The grave itself is a monumental structure, measuring approximately 4 meters in length and 2 meters in width. It consists of a rectangular stone setting, with large stones forming the sides and smaller stones filling the interior. The grave was covered with a mound of earth, creating a distinctive burial mound that was characteristic of Viking burials.

Within the grave, the remains of the Birka Warrior were discovered. The skeletal remains indicated that she was a woman of robust build, estimated to be around 30 to 40 years old at the time of her death. The positioning of the body, with her head to the west and feet to the east, was in accordance with Viking burial customs. The presence of a sword and other weapons alongside her body further emphasized her warrior status.

The grave goods found within the burial mound provide valuable insights into the Birka Warrior's life and status. Among the most notable artifacts are the weapons and armor, which include a sword, spearheads, arrows, and a shield. These weapons were not merely ceremonial, but rather functional and designed for use in battle. The presence of such weaponry suggests that the Birka Warrior was not only a symbol of power and authority but also actively engaged in warfare.

In addition to the weapons, the grave contained a variety of personal items and jewelry. These included a set of gaming pieces, indicating her participation in recreational activities, as well as a comb, indicating her concern for personal grooming. The presence of silver coins and a balance scale suggests involvement in trade and commerce, further highlighting her influential role within the community.

The grave of the Birka Warrior has sparked significant controversy and debate among archaeologists and historians. One of the main controversies surrounding the Birka Warrior is the initial assumption that she was male. This assumption was based on the presence of weapons and the traditional association of such items with male burials. However, subsequent analysis of the skeletal remains and DNA testing confirmed that the Birka Warrior was indeed a woman.

The discovery of a female warrior burial challenged long-held assumptions about gender roles in Viking society. It highlighted the existence of powerful and influential women who not only participated in warfare but also held positions of authority and leadership. This challenges the traditional narrative of Viking society as male-dominated and provides evidence of gender fluidity and flexibility in the Viking Age.

Understanding the Birka Warrior as a female ruler is crucial for a comprehensive understanding of Viking society. It demonstrates that women in Viking society were not confined to traditional gender roles but could actively participate in traditionally male-dominated spheres. The Birka Warrior's burial challenges the notion that women were solely relegated to domestic and nurturing roles, and instead reveals a more complex and diverse social structure.

Furthermore, the discovery of the Birka Warrior's grave highlights the existence of gender fluidity in Viking culture. The presence of weapons and armor traditionally associated with masculinity, alongside personal items and jewelry traditionally associated with femininity, suggests a fluidity and flexibility in gender expression. This challenges the binary understanding of gender and emphasizes the existence of diverse gender identities and roles within Viking society.

The Birka Warrior's grave serves as a powerful reminder that gender fluidity and non-conformity have existed throughout history. It challenges the notion that gender identities and roles are fixed and unchanging, and instead highlights the fluid nature of gender expression. This understanding has important implications for modern society, as it encourages a more inclusive and accepting approach to gender diversity.

In conclusion, the grave of the Birka Warrior provides a

fascinating glimpse into the life of a powerful female ruler in Viking society. The description of the grave, including its structure, the presence of weapons and armor, and the array of personal items and jewelry, offers valuable insights into her status and role within the community. The controversies surrounding the Birka Warrior's gender challenge traditional assumptions and highlight the fluidity of gender roles in Viking society. Understanding the significance of the Birka Warrior as a female ruler and the existence of gender fluidity in Viking culture is essential for a comprehensive understanding of the complexities of gender throughout history.

3.2 Funerary Objects and Artifacts

The funerary objects and artifacts found within the Birka Warrior's grave provide valuable insights into the individual's status, identity, and role within Viking society. These items not only shed light on the material culture of the time but also offer clues about the Birka Warrior's gender and potential position of power.

The grave of the Birka Warrior, discovered in the 19th century on the island of Björkö in Sweden, contained a wealth of artifacts that reflect the individual's high social standing. Among the most notable objects found were weapons, armor, personal items, and jewelry. These items not only showcase the warrior's martial prowess but also provide evidence of their wealth and influence.

One of the most significant funerary objects found in the Birka Warrior's grave is a sword, a symbol of power and authority in Viking society. The sword discovered in the grave was of exceptional quality, indicating the warrior's elite status. Alongside the sword, a shield was also found, further emphasizing the Birka Warrior's role as a skilled combatant. These weapons suggest that the individual held a position of leadership and participated in warfare.

In addition to the weapons, the grave contained a range of personal items and jewelry. These objects included a comb, a spindle whorl, and a gaming board, indicating the Birka Warrior's engagement with daily activities and leisure pursuits. The presence of jewelry, such as brooches, rings, and beads, suggests a desire to display wealth and status. These items were often used as symbols of power and were commonly worn by individuals of high social standing.

The presence of such a diverse array of funerary objects and artifacts challenges traditional gender roles and expectations within Viking society. The assumption that the Birka Warrior was male based solely on the presence of weapons has been called into question. The discovery of female warriors in other Viking burials, as well as the presence of feminine personal items and jewelry in the Birka Warrior's grave, suggests that gender roles in Viking society were more fluid and complex than previously believed.

The controversy surrounding the Birka Warrior's gender highlights the importance of understanding and acknowledging the existence of female leaders and warriors throughout history. By recognizing the Birka Warrior as a female, we challenge the traditional narrative that positions men as the sole participants in warfare and positions of power. This discovery forces us to reevaluate our assumptions about gender roles and the contributions of women in Viking society.

Furthermore, the Birka Warrior's grave provides evidence of gender fluidity in the Viking Age. The presence of both traditionally masculine and feminine objects challenges the notion of fixed gender identities and suggests that individuals in Viking society may have embraced a more fluid understanding of gender. This challenges the idea that gender fluidity is a modern concept and

3.3 Weapons and Armor

The Birka Warrior's grave not only revealed fascinating insights into her gender and identity but also provided valuable information about the weapons and armor she was buried with. These artifacts shed light on her role in Viking society and her status as a warrior. The presence of such weapons and armor challenges traditional gender roles and highlights the fluidity of gender identity in the Viking Age.

The Birka Warrior's grave contained an impressive array of weapons, indicating her proficiency in combat. Among the weapons found were swords, spears, and arrows. Swords were highly prized possessions in Viking society and were often associated with warriors of high status. The presence of multiple swords in the Birka Warrior's grave suggests her elevated position within Viking society. The swords were well-crafted and designed for both offense and defense, indicating her skill and experience in battle.

In addition to swords, the Birka Warrior's grave also contained spears. Spears were versatile weapons used by both infantry and cavalry in Viking warfare. They were effective for thrusting and throwing, making them essential in close combat. The presence of spears in the grave suggests that the Birka Warrior was not only skilled in swordsmanship but also proficient in other forms of combat.

Archaeologists also discovered arrows in the Birka Warrior's grave. Arrows were crucial in long-range combat and were used by both archers and mounted warriors. The presence of arrows indicates that the Birka Warrior was skilled in archery and possibly participated in battles from a distance. This further emphasizes her versatility as a warrior and her ability to adapt to different combat situations.

Alongside the weapons, the Birka Warrior's grave contained various pieces of armor, providing further evidence of her status as a warrior. Armor was essential for protection in battle, and the presence of such items in her grave suggests that she actively engaged in combat. The armor included fragments of chainmail, which was made by interlocking metal rings to form a protective mesh. Chainmail was a highly effective form of armor and was often worn by Viking warriors. Its presence in the Birka Warrior's grave indicates her commitment to personal safety and her understanding of the importance of armor in battle.

The discovery of weapons and armor in the Birka Warrior's grave challenges traditional gender roles and highlights the fluidity of gender identity in Viking society. The assumption that only men were warriors and held positions of power is challenged by the presence of a female warrior buried with such prestigious weapons and armor. This challenges the notion that gender roles were fixed and rigid in the Viking Age.

The Birka Warrior's grave provides evidence that gender fluidity and the acceptance of non-traditional gender roles existed in Viking society. It suggests that individuals were not confined to societal expectations based on their assigned gender. The presence of a female warrior with weapons and armor traditionally associated with men demonstrates that gender roles were more complex and varied than previously believed.

Understanding the Birka Warrior's gender and the significance of her weapons and armor is crucial in unraveling the mysteries of the female ruler. It challenges the traditional narrative of male dominance in Viking society and highlights the importance of recognizing and celebrating the contributions of women in history. The Birka Warrior's story serves as a reminder that gender fluidity has been present throughout history and that individuals have always existed outside of traditional gender norms.

By acknowledging the existence of female warriors like the Birka Warrior, we can challenge and dismantle gender stereotypes that persist in modern society. Her story serves as an inspiration for women and a call for gender equality. It reminds us that women have always been capable of leadership, strength, and bravery, and that their contributions should be recognized and celebrated.

The weapons and armor found in the Birka Warrior's grave not only provide valuable insights into her role as a warrior but also serve as a testament to the fluidity of gender identity in Viking society. They challenge our preconceived notions of gender roles and highlight the importance of embracing diversity and inclusivity in our understanding of history. The Birka Warrior's story continues to inspire and empower individuals today, reminding us of the enduring legacy of female leadership and the ongoing struggle for gender equality.

3.4 Personal Items and Jewelry

The personal items and jewelry found in the grave of the Birka Warrior provide valuable insights into her identity and status within Viking society. These artifacts not only showcase her wealth and power but also shed light on the cultural significance of personal adornment and the role of jewelry in Viking culture.

One of the most striking aspects of the Birka Warrior's grave is the abundance of personal items and jewelry buried with her. These objects include brooches, beads, pendants, rings, and other decorative pieces. The sheer quantity and quality of these artifacts indicate that the Birka Warrior held a position of high status and wealth.

The jewelry found in the grave is a testament to the craftsmanship and artistic skill of the Viking people. The brooches, in particular, are exquisite examples of intricate metalwork, often adorned with intricate patterns and inlaid with precious stones. These brooches were not only functional but also served as symbols of wealth and social standing.

The presence of jewelry in the Birka Warrior's grave also highlights the importance of personal adornment in Viking culture. Jewelry was not only worn for aesthetic purposes but also held symbolic and ritualistic significance. It was believed to possess protective and magical properties, and wearing jewelry was seen as a way to connect with the divine and enhance one's power and status.

The variety of personal items found in the grave suggests that the Birka Warrior had diverse interests and pursuits. For example, gaming pieces and a set of scales indicate her involvement in recreational activities and possibly trade. These objects provide a glimpse into her daily life and activities beyond the battlefield.

The presence of personal items and jewelry in the Birka Warrior's grave challenges traditional gender roles and assumptions about Viking society. The burial of such valuable and significant artifacts with a female individual challenges the notion that women in Viking society were solely confined to domestic roles. It suggests that women could hold positions of power and authority, engage in warfare, and accumulate wealth and prestige.

The discovery of the Birka Warrior and the controversies surrounding her burial have sparked important discussions about gender fluidity and the fluidity of gender roles in the Viking Age. The fact that a woman was buried with weapons and armor traditionally associated with male warriors challenges the binary understanding of gender in Viking society. It suggests that gender roles were not fixed and that individuals could transcend societal expectations.

Understanding the Birka Warrior as a female ruler provides a valuable historical precedent for gender fluidity and challenges the notion that gender identities and expressions are modern constructs. It highlights the existence of diverse gender identities and expressions throughout history and emphasizes the need to recognize and respect these identities in contemporary society.

The Birka Warrior's grave and the personal items and jewelry found within it serve as a powerful reminder of the complexity and diversity of Viking society. They challenge our preconceived notions about gender roles and provide evidence of the fluidity of gender identity and expression in the past. By studying and understanding the significance of these artifacts, we can gain a deeper appreciation for the rich and multifaceted nature of

Viking culture and its relevance to contemporary discussions on gender equality and fluidity.

4

Chapter 4

The Birka Warrior's Identity

4.1 Initial Assumptions and Misconceptions

The discovery of the Birka Warrior, a female Viking warrior buried in the 10th century, challenged long-held assumptions and sparked significant controversies in the field of archaeology. Unearthed in the 19th century at the Viking trading center of Birka, located on the island of Björkö in present-day Sweden, the Birka Warrior's grave contained a wealth of weapons, armor, and other artifacts traditionally associated with male warriors. This unexpected find initially led archaeologists to assume that the individual buried was a man, as it was inconceivable to many that a woman could hold such a prominent warrior role in Viking society.

The controversies surrounding the Birka Warrior primarily revolve around the initial misinterpretation of the burial and the subsequent resistance to accepting the possibility of a female warrior. When the grave was first excavated, the assumption that it belonged to a male warrior was based on the presence of weapons and the belief that women did not participate in combat during the Viking Age. These assumptions were deeply rooted in gender stereotypes and societal expectations, which influenced the interpretation of archaeological findings.

The significance of recognizing the Birka Warrior as a female challenges the traditional narrative of Viking society and high-lights the existence of gender fluidity throughout history. By acknowledging that women could hold positions of power and engage in warfare, we gain a more nuanced understanding of gender roles in the past. This discovery forces us to question preconceived notions about gender and challenges the idea that gender roles have always been rigidly defined.

The Birka Warrior's burial provides evidence that gender flu-idity was present in Viking society. It suggests that individuals were not confined to strict gender roles and that the expression of gender identity was more diverse than previously assumed. The presence of a female warrior challenges the notion that gender was solely determined by biological sex and highlights the fluidity of gender identity in the Viking Age.

Understanding the existence of gender fluidity in the past is crucial for several reasons. Firstly, it allows us to challenge and deconstruct modern-day assumptions about gender roles and expectations. By recognizing that gender fluidity has been present throughout history, we can move away from rigid gender norms and embrace a more inclusive and accepting society.

Secondly, acknowledging the Birka Warrior as a female ruler provides historical precedent for women in positions of power. It challenges the notion that women were solely confined to domestic roles and demonstrates that they could hold positions of authority and leadership. This challenges the patriarchal narrative that has dominated historical accounts and empowers women by providing them with historical role models.

Furthermore, the discovery of the Birka Warrior emphasizes the importance of reevaluating archaeological interpretations and challenging biases within the field. It serves as a reminder that assumptions and misconceptions can hinder our understanding of the past. By critically examining archaeological evidence and questioning preconceived notions, we can uncover hidden narratives and gain a more accurate understanding of historical events.

The Birka Warrior's burial challenges the traditional narrative of Viking society and highlights the complexity of gender roles in the past. It serves as a powerful reminder that gender fluidity has existed for centuries and that our understanding of gender is not fixed or universal. By embracing the diversity of gender identities and challenging societal expectations, we can create a more inclusive and equitable future. The Birka Warrior's story is a testament to the resilience and strength of individuals who defy societal norms and pave the way for greater acceptance and understanding.

4.2 Reevaluating Gender in Archaeology

The discovery of the Birka Warrior, a female Viking warrior buried with weapons and armor, has sparked significant controversy and reevaluation of gender roles in archaeology. This section will delve into the complexities of gender in archaeological interpretations and shed light on the significance of the Birka Warrior's gender.

Archaeology, like many other disciplines, has traditionally

been influenced by societal norms and biases, often assuming that certain artifacts or burial practices are associated with specific genders. This has led to the misinterpretation or exclusion of women's roles and contributions in the past. The Birka Warrior's burial challenges these assumptions and forces a reevaluation of gender in archaeology.

The Birka Warrior was discovered in the late 19th century by Swedish archaeologist Hjalmar Stolpe during excavations at the Viking Age trading center of Birka, located on the island of Björkö in present-day Sweden. The burial site, known as Bj 581, contained a rich array of grave goods, including weapons, armor, and other personal items typically associated with male warriors.

Controversy surrounding the Birka Warrior primarily stems from the initial assumption that the burial belonged to a male warrior. This assumption was based on the presence of weapons and the belief that women in Viking society were not involved in combat. However, subsequent osteological analysis revealed that the individual buried in Bj 581 was biologically female, challenging the traditional understanding of gender roles in Viking society.

The significance of the Birka Warrior's gender lies in the fact that it disrupts long-held assumptions about the roles and capabilities of women in the Viking Age. It highlights the need to reevaluate gender in archaeological interpretations and recognize the diversity of experiences and contributions of individuals in the past. The Birka Warrior's burial demonstrates that women were not confined to traditional gender roles and were capable of participating in warfare and holding positions of power.

Furthermore, the discovery of the Birka Warrior supports

the idea that gender fluidity has existed throughout history. Gender fluidity refers to the concept that gender is not fixed and can change or be expressed in various ways. In Viking society, gender roles were not as rigidly defined as in some other cultures, allowing for more fluid expressions of gender identity.

The existence of the Birka Warrior challenges the notion that gender fluidity is a modern phenomenon. It suggests that societies in the past recognized and accepted a broader spectrum of gender identities and expressions. By acknowledging the presence of gender fluidity in the Viking Age, we gain a deeper understanding of the complexities of human experiences and challenge the notion that gender is a binary construct.

Understanding the presence of gender fluidity in the past has important implications for modern society. It challenges the rigid gender norms and stereotypes that persist today and promotes inclusivity and acceptance of diverse gender identities. The Birka Warrior's burial serves as a powerful reminder that gender diversity has always been a part of human history and should be celebrated and respected.

Reevaluating gender in archaeology requires a shift in perspective and a willingness to challenge preconceived notions. It involves critically examining archaeological evidence and considering alternative interpretations that may have been overlooked in the past. The discovery of the Birka Warrior serves as a catalyst for this reevaluation and encourages archaeologists to approach gender in their research with a more open and inclusive mindset.

In conclusion, the Birka Warrior's burial challenges traditional assumptions about gender roles in Viking society and highlights the presence of gender fluidity in the past. Reevaluating gender in archaeology is crucial for a more accurate understanding of the past and for promoting inclusivity and acceptance in the present. The Birka Warrior's story serves as a powerful reminder of the enduring nature of gender diversity and its importance in shaping human history.

4.3 The Birka Warrior as a Female Ruler

The discovery of the Birka Warrior, a female buried with weapons and armor traditionally associated with male warriors, has sparked significant controversy and debate among archaeologists and historians. Unearthed in the 19th century at the Viking Age trading center of Birka in Sweden, this burial site challenges long-held assumptions about gender roles in Viking society. The presence of a female buried with such prestigious grave goods raises questions about the Birka Warrior's identity and the role of women in Viking culture.

The controversy surrounding the Birka Warrior primarily stems from the initial assumption that the individual buried was male. When the grave was first excavated, the presence of weapons and armor led archaeologists to conclude that the burial belonged to a high-ranking male warrior. However, subsequent osteological analysis revealed that the remains belonged to a biological female. This revelation challenged the prevailing notion that women in Viking society were primarily confined to domestic roles and had limited participation in warfare.

Understanding the Birka Warrior as a female ruler is crucial for several reasons. Firstly, it challenges the traditional narrative that positions men as the sole wielders of power and authority in Viking society. By recognizing the Birka Warrior as a female ruler, we acknowledge the existence of women who held positions of leadership and influence. This challenges the notion that women were passive participants in Viking society and highlights the complexity and diversity of gender roles during that time.

Furthermore, the Birka Warrior's burial challenges the binary understanding of gender prevalent in many historical and archaeological interpretations. It demonstrates that gender fluidity and non-conformity have existed throughout history, even in societies that are often perceived as rigidly patriarchal. The presence of a female buried with weapons and armor suggests that gender roles in Viking society were more nuanced and flexible than previously assumed.

The Birka Warrior's burial also sheds light on the interconnectedness of gender and power dynamics in Viking society. As a female ruler, she would have faced unique challenges and navigated complex social structures. Her ability to command respect and authority in a society dominated by men speaks to her exceptional leadership qualities and the recognition she received from her contemporaries.

To fully understand the Birka Warrior's significance as a female ruler, it is essential to consider the historical context in which she lived. Viking society was characterized by a decentralized political structure, with power often distributed among local chieftains and rulers. Women in Viking society had more agency and autonomy compared to their counterparts in other contemporary societies. They could inherit property, engage in trade, and participate in decision-making processes. The Birka Warrior's burial reflects the existence of powerful women who actively participated in political and military affairs.

The Birka Warrior's story serves as an inspiration for women and a reminder of the long history of female leadership and empowerment. Her burial challenges societal norms and expectations, highlighting the potential for women to break free from traditional gender roles and excel in positions of power. By recognizing the Birka Warrior as a female ruler, we acknowledge the contributions and capabilities of women throughout history, promoting gender equality and dismantling gender stereotypes.

Moreover, the Birka Warrior's burial provides valuable insights into the fluidity of gender identity in Viking culture. It demonstrates that gender roles were not fixed or rigidly defined but could be negotiated and adapted based on individual circumstances and societal needs. This challenges the notion that gender fluidity is a recent phenomenon and emphasizes that diverse gender expressions have existed for centuries.

The Birka Warrior's story also underscores the importance of interdisciplinary research and the need to reevaluate assumptions in archaeology and gender studies. It serves as a reminder that our understanding of the past is constantly evolving, and new discoveries can challenge established narratives. The Birka Warrior's burial has prompted scholars to reconsider their interpretations of gender in Viking society and has opened up new avenues for research and exploration.

In conclusion, the Birka Warrior's identification as a female ruler challenges traditional notions of gender roles in Viking society and highlights the fluidity of gender identity. Recognizing her as a powerful leader provides a more nuanced understanding of Viking culture and promotes gender equality. The Birka Warrior's story serves as an inspiration for women and a reminder of the long history of female empowerment. Her burial encourages us to question societal norms and expectations, promoting a more inclusive and diverse understanding of gender in both the past and present.

4.4 Historical Context and Power Dynamics

The discovery of the Birka Warrior has sparked significant interest and debate among historians, archaeologists, and gender scholars. To fully understand the historical context and power dynamics surrounding this remarkable find, it is crucial to delve into the broader societal and political landscape of the Viking Age.

The Viking Age, spanning from the late 8th to the 11th century, was a time of exploration, expansion, and cultural exchange for the Norse people. During this period, Viking society was predominantly patriarchal, with men holding positions of power and authority. However, recent archaeological discoveries, including the Birka Warrior, have challenged these assumptions and shed light on the complex dynamics of gender and power in Viking society.

The Birka Warrior, a burial site discovered in the 19th century on the island of Björkö in Sweden, contained the remains of a high-status individual accompanied by an array of weapons, armor, and other grave goods traditionally associated with male warriors. Initially, the assumption was that the individual buried at Birka was a male warrior, as this aligned with prevailing gender norms of the time. However, subsequent osteological analysis and DNA testing revealed that the Birka Warrior was, in fact, a biological female.

This revelation has sparked controversies and debates surrounding the Birka Warrior's identity and the implications of her gender. Some skeptics argue that the burial may have been a mistake or that the individual was merely a woman buried with weapons as a symbol of status. However, the presence of a diverse range of weapons, including swords, arrows, and shields, suggests that the Birka Warrior was not merely a passive participant in warfare but an active combatant.

Understanding the Birka Warrior as a female warrior challenges traditional notions of gender roles and power dynamics in Viking society. It highlights the existence of women who defied societal expectations and actively participated in warfare, potentially holding positions of authority and leadership. This challenges the prevailing narrative that Viking women were primarily confined to domestic roles and were passive participants in the male-dominated sphere of warfare.

The Birka Warrior's existence also provides evidence of gender fluidity and the acceptance of diverse gender expressions in Viking society. While the Birka Warrior's gender identity may never be fully known, her burial with traditionally masculine grave goods suggests that she may have adopted a gender role typically associated with men. This challenges the binary understanding of gender and highlights the fluidity and complexity of gender identities throughout history.

The acceptance of gender fluidity in Viking society is further supported by historical accounts and sagas that mention female warriors, known as shieldmaidens. These shieldmaidens were revered for their bravery and skill in battle, challenging the notion that women were solely passive participants in Viking warfare. The existence of the Birka Warrior aligns with these historical accounts and provides tangible evidence of the presence of female warriors in Viking society.

Understanding the historical context and power dynamics surrounding the Birka Warrior is crucial for gaining insights into the broader social structure of Viking society. It suggests that women in positions of power and authority were not entirely un-heard of and that gender roles were more fluid and diverse than previously assumed. This challenges the traditional narrative of male dominance and female subordination in Viking society and highlights the need for a more nuanced understanding of gender dynamics in the past.

The Birka Warrior's story serves as a powerful reminder that gender fluidity and the existence of female leaders are not recent phenomena. It demonstrates that societies throughout history have grappled with complex understandings of gender and that women have played significant roles in shaping political, social, and military landscapes. By acknowledging and celebrating the Birka Warrior's existence, we can draw inspiration for promoting gender equality and challenging gender norms in our own time.

5

Chapter 5

Female Warriors in Viking Society

5.1 Historical Accounts of Female Warriors

Throughout history, there have been numerous accounts of female warriors who defied societal norms and played active roles in warfare. These accounts provide valuable insights into the diverse roles and capabilities of women in different cultures and time periods. The discovery of the Birka Warrior, a female Viking warrior buried in the 10th century, adds to this rich tapestry of historical accounts.

The Birka Warrior, also known as the "Birka female Viking warrior," was found in the late 19th century during archaeological excavations at the Viking trading center of Birka, located on the island of Björkö in present-day Sweden. The burial site of the Birka Warrior, known as grave Bj 581, contained a wealth of grave goods and artifacts typically associated with high-ranking warriors, including weapons, armor, and personal items.

The discovery of a female buried with such prestigious grave goods sparked controversy and debate among archaeologists and historians. For many years, the assumption was that the Birka Warrior must have been a male, as the presence of weapons and armor was traditionally associated with male warriors. However, subsequent analysis of the skeletal remains and DNA testing confirmed that the Birka Warrior was indeed a female.

The controversy surrounding the Birka Warrior stems from the prevailing gender norms and expectations of Viking society. The traditional view of Viking society portrayed men as the primary warriors and women as passive participants in domestic and reproductive roles. The discovery of a female warrior challenges these preconceived notions and forces a reevaluation of gender roles in Viking society.

Understanding that the Birka Warrior was a female is significant because it highlights the existence of female warriors in Viking society and challenges the notion that women were solely confined to domestic roles. It provides evidence that women in Viking society had agency and were capable of participating in warfare, a traditionally male-dominated sphere.

Furthermore, the discovery of the Birka Warrior supports the idea that gender fluidity has been present throughout history. Gender fluidity refers to the concept that gender is not fixed and can vary over time and across different cultures. The existence of female warriors in Viking society suggests that gender roles were not rigidly defined and that individuals had the freedom to express their gender identity in various ways.

The Birka Warrior's burial site and the grave goods found within it provide valuable insights into the role of female warriors in Viking society. The presence of weapons and armor suggests that the Birka Warrior was not merely a symbolic figure but actively participated in battle. This challenges the notion that female warriors were rare exceptions and suggests that they played a more significant role in Viking warfare than previously believed.

Historical accounts of female warriors in Viking society are not limited to the Birka Warrior. Sagas and other written sources from the Viking Age also mention female warriors, known as shieldmaidens. These shieldmaidens were skilled fighters who accompanied Viking armies and participated in battles alongside their male counterparts. While the exact extent of their involvement in warfare is debated, their existence in historical accounts further supports the idea that women had active roles in Viking warfare.

The historical accounts of female warriors in Viking society provide a more nuanced understanding of gender dynamics in the past. They challenge the notion that women were passive participants in Viking society and highlight the agency and capabilities of women in a traditionally male-dominated sphere. These accounts also demonstrate that gender fluidity has been present throughout history, further emphasizing the importance of recognizing and respecting diverse gender identities in contemporary society.

5.2 Shieldmaidens

The concept of shieldmaidens, or female warriors, has long captured the imagination of people throughout history. These legendary figures, often depicted as fierce and skilled fighters, have been a subject of fascination and debate. The discovery of the Birka Warrior, a female Viking buried with weapons and armor, has reignited discussions surrounding the existence and role of shieldmaidens in Viking society.

The Birka Warrior, also known as Grave Bj 581, was found in the 19th century during archaeological excavations at the Viking trading center of Birka, located on the island of Björkö in present-day Sweden. The burial site, dated to the 10th century, contained a rich array of grave goods, including weapons, armor, and personal items typically associated with high-ranking warriors. The presence of these items initially led archaeologists to assume that the individual buried there was a male warrior.

However, in recent years, a reevaluation of the Birka Warrior's remains and grave goods has challenged this assumption. Through the use of osteological analysis and DNA testing, it was determined that the individual was, in fact, a biological female. This revelation has sparked controversy and debate within the archaeological community and beyond.

One of the main controversies surrounding the Birka Warrior revolves around the interpretation of her burial as evidence of female warriors in Viking society. Skeptics argue that the presence of weapons and armor in her grave may not necessarily indicate her role as a warrior. They suggest that these items could have been symbolic or ceremonial in nature, rather than indicative of her actual combat involvement. However, proponents of the shieldmaiden theory argue that the presence of such elaborate weaponry and defensive equipment suggests a high level of martial skill and participation in warfare.

Understanding the Birka Warrior's gender is crucial in challenging traditional assumptions about gender roles in Viking society. The prevailing image of Vikings as exclusively male warriors has been deeply ingrained in popular culture and historical narratives. The discovery of a female warrior challenges this stereotype and highlights the complexity and diversity of gender roles in the Viking Age.

The existence of female warriors, such as the Birka Warrior, also sheds light on the concept of gender fluidity in historical societies. Gender fluidity refers to the idea that gender identities and expressions can change and vary over time. The presence of female warriors in Viking society suggests that gender roles were not fixed or rigid, but rather fluid and adaptable.

The Birka Warrior's burial challenges the notion that gender roles in the past were strictly defined and limited. It suggests that women in Viking society had the agency to participate in traditionally male-dominated activities, such as warfare. This challenges the binary understanding of gender and highlights the existence of diverse gender identities and expressions in the past.

The recognition of gender fluidity in historical societies has important implications for our understanding of gender today. It challenges the notion that gender is solely determined by biological sex and highlights the social and cultural aspects of gender identity. By acknowledging the existence of female warriors like the Birka Warrior, we can challenge gender norms and stereotypes that limit individuals based on their assigned sex.

The Birka Warrior's story serves as a powerful reminder that gender fluidity and the existence of female warriors are not recent phenomena. They have been present throughout history, even in societies that are often portrayed as strictly patriarchal. By uncovering and understanding these historical examples, we can challenge and dismantle gender stereotypes, promoting greater inclusivity and equality in our own society. The Birka Warrior's legacy serves as an inspiration for women and a testament to the enduring fight for gender equality.

5.3 Women in Viking Warfare

Throughout history, the role of women in warfare has often been overlooked or downplayed. However, recent archaeological discoveries, such as the Birka Warrior, have shed light on the significant contributions of women in Viking society. The Birka Warrior, a female ruler buried with weapons and armor, challenges traditional notions of gender roles and highlights the presence of women in Viking warfare.

The discovery of the Birka Warrior in the late 19th century at the Viking trading center of Birka, located on the island of Björkö in present-day Sweden, caused a stir in the archaeological community. The burial site, known as Bj 581, contained a rich array of grave goods, including swords, spears, shields, and a full suit of armor. Initially, the assumption was that the individual buried in this elaborate grave was a male warrior. However, subsequent osteological analysis revealed that the Birka Warrior was, in fact, a woman.

This revelation sparked controversy and debate among scholars. Some argued that the presence of weapons and armor in the grave indicated that the Birka Warrior held a high-ranking military position. Others questioned the interpretation, suggesting that the grave goods might have been symbolic or ceremonial rather than indicative of actual combat involvement. The controversy surrounding the Birka Warrior's gender highlights the biases and assumptions that have historically influenced archaeological interpretations.

Understanding that the Birka Warrior was a female is crucial for several reasons. Firstly, it challenges the prevailing narrative that women in Viking society were primarily confined to domestic roles. The presence of a female warrior suggests that women had agency and could participate in traditionally male-dominated spheres, such as warfare. This challenges the notion that gender roles were fixed and rigid in Viking society.

Furthermore, the discovery of the Birka Warrior supports the idea that gender fluidity has existed throughout history. Gender fluidity refers to the concept that gender is not strictly binary but exists on a spectrum. In Viking society, gender roles were more fluid and flexible than in many other contemporary cultures. The presence of female warriors, such as the Birka Warrior, suggests that gender was not solely determined by biological sex but could be influenced by social and cultural factors.

The Birka Warrior's burial site provides evidence of the acceptance and recognition of women in positions of power and authority within Viking society. The presence of weapons and armor in her grave indicates that she held a significant military role. This challenges the notion that women were solely relegated to passive roles in Viking society and highlights the importance of female leadership and participation in warfare.

By acknowledging the existence of female warriors in Viking society, we gain a more nuanced understanding of gender dynamics in the past. It allows us to move beyond simplistic and binary notions of gender and recognize the diversity of experiences and roles that individuals could occupy. The Birka Warrior's story serves as a reminder that gender roles are not fixed or universal but are shaped by cultural and historical contexts.

The recognition of the Birka Warrior as a female ruler also has implications for contemporary society. It challenges traditional gender norms and stereotypes, encouraging a more inclusive and diverse understanding of leadership and power. The Birka Warrior's story serves as an inspiration for women and girls, demonstrating that they have the potential to excel in traditionally male-dominated fields and break down barriers.

In conclusion, the discovery of the Birka Warrior and other female warriors in Viking society has shattered long-held assumptions about gender roles in the past. The presence of women in Viking warfare challenges traditional narratives and highlights the fluidity of gender identity and expression. Understanding the role of women in Viking warfare provides valuable insights into the complexity of gender dynamics and serves as a source of inspiration for promoting gender equality in the present day.

5.4 The Birka Warrior's Role in Battle

The discovery of the Birka Warrior has sparked numerous debates and controversies surrounding her identity and role in Viking society. While the burial site itself provides valuable insights into her status and wealth, it is her gender that has captured the attention of scholars and historians. Understanding the Birka Warrior's role in battle is crucial in unraveling the complexities of gender fluidity and challenging traditional notions of gender roles in history.

The Birka Warrior, believed to be a female ruler, was found in the 19th century during archaeological excavations at Birka, an important Viking trading center in present-day Sweden. The burial site, known as Bj 581, contained a rich array of grave goods and artifacts, including weapons, armor, personal items, and jewelry. These findings initially led archaeologists to assume that the individual buried there was a high-ranking male warrior.

However, in recent years, advancements in archaeological

techniques, such as DNA analysis, have revealed that the Birka Warrior was, in fact, a woman. This revelation has challenged long-held assumptions about gender roles in Viking society and has sparked intense debates among scholars. Some have argued that the burial may have been an exception, while others suggest that female warriors were more common than previously believed.

The Birka Warrior's role in battle is a topic of great interest and speculation. While the presence of weapons and armor in her grave suggests a connection to warfare, the exact nature of her involvement remains uncertain. It is important to note that the Birka Warrior's burial is unique, and there is limited evidence to draw definitive conclusions about her specific role in battle. However, it is clear that she held a position of power and authority within Viking society.

The existence of female warriors in Viking society is not entirely surprising. Historical accounts and sagas mention the presence of shieldmaidens, women who fought alongside men in battle. These accounts, although often dismissed as myth or exaggeration, provide glimpses into the complex and varied roles women played in Viking warfare.

The Birka Warrior's burial challenges the notion that women were solely relegated to domestic and nurturing roles in Viking society. Her presence as a high-ranking warrior suggests that women could attain positions of authority and respect in a society traditionally associated with male dominance. This challenges the binary understanding of gender roles and highlights the fluidity of gender identity in the Viking Age.

The Birka Warrior's role in battle also sheds light on the broader concept of gender fluidity throughout history. It demonstrates that the acceptance and recognition of diverse gender identities and expressions are not recent phenomena but have existed for centuries. The existence of female warriors in Viking society challenges the notion that gender roles are fixed and unchanging, emphasizing the fluidity and complexity of gender throughout human history.

Understanding the Birka Warrior's role in battle is crucial in dismantling gender stereotypes and promoting gender equality. Her story serves as a powerful reminder that women have always been capable of strength, courage, and leadership. By acknowledging and celebrating the Birka Warrior's accomplishments, we can inspire women and girls today to pursue their ambitions and challenge societal expectations.

Furthermore, the Birka Warrior's story provides historical validation for individuals who identify as non-binary, transgender, or gender non-conforming. It demonstrates that diverse gender identities have always existed and have been recognized in different cultures throughout history. By acknowledging the Birka Warrior's gender identity, we can foster a more inclusive and accepting society that embraces the full spectrum of gender diversity.

In conclusion, the Birka Warrior's role in battle is a subject of ongoing research and debate. While her exact involvement in warfare remains uncertain, her burial site and the presence of weapons and armor indicate her high status and authority. The Birka Warrior's story challenges traditional gender roles, highlights the fluidity of gender identity in the Viking Age, and serves as an inspiration for women and gender equality. By understanding and celebrating her legacy, we can continue to challenge societal norms and promote a more inclusive understanding of gender throughout history.

6

Chapter 6

The Birka Warrior's Life and Legacy

6.1 Possible Life Story of the Birka Warrior

The Birka Warrior, a remarkable figure from the Viking Age, continues to captivate the imagination of historians, archaeologists, and enthusiasts alike. While we may never know the exact details of her life, it is possible to construct a possible life story based on the evidence surrounding her burial and the historical context of the time.

The Birka Warrior, also known as Grave Bj 581, was discovered in the late 19th century by Swedish archaeologist Hjalmar Stolpe during excavations at the Viking trading center of Birka, located on the island of Björkö in present-day Sweden. The burial site, dating back to the 10th century, contained a wealth of grave goods and artifacts, including weapons, armor, personal items, and jewelry.

Controversies surrounding the Birka Warrior primarily revolve around her gender. Initially, the assumption was made that the individual buried with such prestigious grave goods must have been a male warrior. However, upon closer examination and reevaluation of the evidence, it became clear that the Birka Warrior was, in fact, a woman. This revelation challenged long-held assumptions about gender roles in Viking society and sparked debates among scholars.

Understanding that the Birka Warrior was a female is of utmost importance as it challenges the traditional narrative of male dominance in Viking warfare and leadership. It highlights the existence of powerful women who defied societal norms and played significant roles in Viking society. By acknowledging the Birka Warrior's gender, we gain a more accurate understanding of the diversity and complexity of Viking culture.

The discovery of the Birka Warrior also sheds light on the concept of gender fluidity in history. While the term "gender fluidity" may be a modern construct, the existence of individuals who defied traditional gender roles and expressions is not a new phenomenon. The Birka Warrior's burial challenges the notion that gender roles were fixed and rigid in the Viking Age. It suggests that individuals may have had the freedom to express their gender identity and pursue roles traditionally associated with the opposite sex.

In Viking society, gender roles were not as strictly defined as in many other cultures of the time. Women had more agency and autonomy compared to their counterparts in other societies. They could inherit property, engage in trade, and participate in decision-making processes. The Birka Warrior's burial provides evidence of a woman who not only participated in warfare but also held a position of power and authority.

Based on the evidence, it is possible to speculate on the life story of the Birka Warrior. She may have been born into a noble family, where she received training in combat and leadership from an early age. As she grew older, she likely honed her skills and gained respect within her community. Her prowess in battle and her ability to lead may have earned her the title of a warrior and a ruler.

The Birka Warrior's life would have been filled with challenges and triumphs. She would have navigated the complex web of Viking politics, engaging in trade and diplomacy to secure the prosperity and safety of her people. Her leadership would have been tested in times of conflict, where she would have led her warriors into battle, defending her lands and expanding her influence.

The legacy of the Birka Warrior extends beyond her own life. Her story serves as a reminder of the strength and resilience of women throughout history. It challenges the notion that women were passive participants in Viking society and highlights their contributions to warfare, governance, and trade.

The Birka Warrior's story also serves as an inspiration for women and advocates of gender equality today. It reminds us that women have always been capable of leadership and that gender should never be a barrier to achieving one's goals. By embracing the Birka Warrior's story, we can challenge societal norms and strive for a more inclusive and equitable world.

In conclusion, while we can only speculate about the exact details of the Birka Warrior's life, her burial site and the historical context of the Viking Age provide valuable insights into her possible life story. Understanding her as a female ruler challenges traditional gender roles and highlights the existence of gender fluidity in Viking society. The Birka Warrior's story serves as a powerful reminder of the strength and agency of women throughout history and continues to inspire and empower individuals today.

6.2 Leadership and Governance

The discovery of the Birka Warrior has sparked numerous debates and controversies surrounding her identity and significance. While the focus has primarily been on her gender, it is essential to delve deeper into her role in leadership and governance within Viking society. By examining the historical context and power dynamics of the time, we can gain a better understanding of the Birka Warrior's position and influence.

Leadership in Viking society was often associated with military prowess and the ability to command and protect one's community. It is important to note that leadership roles were not exclusively reserved for men. Women in Viking society had opportunities to exercise power and authority, particularly in times of conflict or absence of male leaders. The Birka Warrior's burial site, with its rich array of weapons and armor, suggests a prominent role in warfare and defense.

In Viking society, governance was often decentralized, with power distributed among local chieftains and rulers. These leaders were responsible for maintaining order, resolving disputes, and overseeing economic activities. The Birka Warrior's grave, located in a prominent position within the Birka settlement, indicates her high status and potential involvement in governance.

While the exact nature of the Birka Warrior's leadership and governance remains speculative, it is plausible to consider her as a ruler or influential figure within her community. Her burial site, with its opulent grave goods and strategic location, suggests a position of authority and respect. It is possible that she held a role similar to that of a chieftain or a regional ruler, responsible for making decisions that affected the lives of those under her rule.

The Birka Warrior's leadership and governance would have encompassed various aspects of Viking society, including trade and diplomacy. The Viking Age was characterized by extensive trade networks, and Birka, as a major trading center, played a crucial role in facilitating economic exchanges. As a leader, the Birka Warrior would have been involved in overseeing and regulating trade activities, ensuring the prosperity and security of her community.

Diplomacy was also an essential aspect of Viking governance. Leaders engaged in negotiations and alliances with neighboring communities, both for economic and defensive purposes. The Birka Warrior, with her military prowess and high status, would have been a key figure in diplomatic relations, representing her community's interests and forging alliances to ensure their safety and prosperity.

Understanding the Birka Warrior's leadership and governance is crucial for comprehending the complexities of Viking society and challenging traditional gender roles. Her existence challenges the notion that leadership and authority were exclusively male domains. By acknowledging her as a female ruler, we recognize the agency and power that women held in Viking society.

The Birka Warrior's story also highlights the fluidity of gender identity in the past. While she may have been assigned female at birth, her adoption of traditionally masculine roles and her burial with weapons and armor suggest a more complex understanding of gender in Viking society. This challenges the binary understanding of gender and emphasizes that gender fluidity has existed throughout history.

By examining the Birka Warrior's leadership and governance, we gain insights into the diverse roles and responsibilities that women held in Viking society. Her story serves as a reminder that gender norms and expectations are not fixed but shaped by cultural and historical contexts. It encourages us to question and challenge our own assumptions about gender roles and to recognize the agency and capabilities of individuals beyond traditional gender boundaries.

The Birka Warrior's legacy extends beyond her own time. Her story inspires women today to embrace leadership roles and challenge societal expectations. It serves as a symbol of empowerment and resilience, reminding us that women have always been capable of wielding power and influencing their communities.

In conclusion, the Birka Warrior's leadership and governance provide a fascinating glimpse into the complexities of Viking society. By recognizing her as a female ruler, we challenge traditional gender roles and highlight the fluidity of gender identity in the past. Her story serves as an inspiration for women today and underscores the importance of understanding and embracing diverse forms of leadership and governance.

6.3 Trade and Diplomacy

Trade and diplomacy played crucial roles in the Viking Age, and the Birka Warrior likely had a significant impact in these areas. As a prominent figure in Viking society, her position as a female ruler would have influenced trade networks, political alliances, and cultural exchanges. Understanding the Birka Warrior's involvement in trade and diplomacy provides valuable insights into the interconnectedness of Viking societies and the role of women in these spheres.

Trade was a fundamental aspect of Viking society, and the Birka Warrior's position of power would have allowed her to engage in and shape these economic activities. Birka, the bustling trading center where she was buried, was a hub for long-distance trade routes, connecting Scandinavia with the wider world. The strategic location of Birka on the island of Björkö in Lake Mälaren made it an ideal site for trade, as it provided access to both the Baltic Sea and the interior of Scandinavia.

The Birka Warrior's burial site, with its rich array of grave goods, suggests her involvement in trade. The presence of exotic objects from distant lands, such as Byzantine coins and Islamic jewelry, indicates her participation in long-distance trade networks. These goods would have been acquired through extensive trade routes and diplomatic connections, highlighting the Birka Warrior's role as a key player in the economic exchanges of the Viking Age.

Diplomacy was another crucial aspect of Viking society, and the Birka Warrior's position as a female ruler would have influenced political alliances and negotiations. The Viking Age was characterized by both conflict and cooperation, and diplomacy played a vital role in maintaining stability and securing advantageous trade agreements. As a powerful leader, the Birka Warrior would have been involved in forging alliances, negotiating treaties, and resolving disputes.

The Birka Warrior's burial site provides evidence of her diplomatic connections. The presence of prestigious gifts from other regions, such as Frankish swords and Anglo-Saxon brooches, suggests her involvement in diplomatic exchanges. These objects would have been bestowed upon her as symbols of friendship, alliance, or tribute, highlighting her role as a respected and influential figure in Viking society.

The Birka Warrior's gender is significant in understanding the dynamics of trade and diplomacy in the Viking Age. While women in many societies were often excluded from positions of power and influence, the Birka Warrior's existence challenges these assumptions. Her role as a female ruler demonstrates that women could hold positions of authority and actively participate in trade and diplomatic activities.

The Birka Warrior's story also highlights the fluidity of gender identity in Viking society. The fact that she was buried with weapons and armor traditionally associated with male warriors challenges the binary understanding of gender roles. It suggests that gender in the Viking Age was not strictly defined and that individuals could occupy roles and express identities that did not conform to societal norms.

Understanding the Birka Warrior as a female ruler involved in trade and diplomacy expands our knowledge of gender dynamics in the Viking Age. It challenges the traditional narrative that positions women solely as passive participants in domestic and familial spheres. Instead, it reveals the agency and influence that women could wield in economic and political arenas.

Furthermore, recognizing the Birka Warrior's gender fluidity emphasizes that the concept of gender as a fixed and binary construct is not universal or timeless. It highlights that societies throughout history have recognized and accommodated diverse gender identities and expressions. The Birka Warrior's story serves as a reminder that gender fluidity has existed for centuries and that it is an integral part of human history.

By studying the Birka Warrior's involvement in trade and

diplomacy, we gain a deeper understanding of the interconnectedness of Viking societies and the multifaceted roles that women played. It challenges preconceived notions about gender and power dynamics in the past and encourages us to reevaluate our understanding of gender in the present. The Birka Warrior's story serves as an inspiration for embracing diversity and promoting gender equality in contemporary society.

6.4 The Birka Warrior's Influence on Viking Society

The discovery of the Birka Warrior has had a profound impact on our understanding of Viking society and the role of women within it. Unveiling the mysteries surrounding this female ruler has challenged traditional notions of gender roles and shed light on the fluidity of gender identity in the Viking Age. The Birka Warrior's influence on Viking society can be seen in various aspects, including social dynamics, power structures, and cultural perceptions.

One of the most significant contributions of the Birka Warrior's discovery is the reevaluation of gender norms and stereotypes in Viking society. Prior to this discovery, the prevailing assumption was that women in the Viking Age were primarily confined to domestic roles and had limited participation in public life. The presence of a female ruler buried with weapons and armor at Birka challenges this assumption and suggests that women held positions of power and authority.

The Birka Warrior's burial site also provides insights into the leadership and governance structures of Viking society. The presence of weapons and armor in the grave suggests that the Birka Warrior was not only a ruler but also a military leader. This challenges the notion that women were solely responsible for nurturing and homemaking, highlighting their active involvement in warfare and decision-making processes.

Furthermore, the Birka Warrior's influence extends to trade and diplomacy. Birka was a significant trading center during the Viking Age, and the presence of a female ruler suggests that women played a crucial role in economic activities and diplomatic relations. The Birka Warrior's burial with valuable personal items and jewelry indicates her involvement in trade networks and her ability to negotiate and maintain alliances.

The Birka Warrior's influence on Viking society goes beyond her individual achievements. Her existence challenges the traditional binary understanding of gender and highlights the fluidity of gender identity in the Viking Age. The presence of a female ruler buried with traditionally masculine objects suggests that gender roles were not fixed and that individuals could express their gender in diverse ways.

Understanding the Birka Warrior as a female ruler also emphasizes the importance of recognizing and celebrating the contributions of women throughout history. By acknowledging the existence of powerful women in Viking society, we can challenge the patriarchal narratives that have dominated historical accounts. This recognition is crucial for promoting gender equality and empowering women in contemporary society.

The Birka Warrior's story serves as an inspiration for women and advocates of gender equality. Her existence demonstrates that women have always been capable of leadership, strength, and courage. By reclaiming the history of female rulers and warriors, we can challenge societal expectations and stereotypes that limit women's potential.

Moreover, the Birka Warrior's influence extends beyond Viking society. Her discovery has sparked discussions and debates in various academic disciplines, including archaeology, history, and gender studies. Scholars and researchers have been prompted to reevaluate their assumptions and methodologies when interpreting gender in the past. This ongoing research and exploration will undoubtedly lead to further discoveries and a deeper understanding of gender fluidity throughout history.

In conclusion, the Birka Warrior's influence on Viking society is far-reaching and multifaceted. Her existence challenges traditional gender roles, provides insights into leadership and governance, and highlights the fluidity of gender identity in the Viking Age. Understanding the Birka Warrior's story is not only important for our understanding of the past but also for inspiring and empowering women in the present. By recognizing and celebrating the contributions of women throughout history, we can strive for a more inclusive and equitable society.

7

Chapter 7

Gender Fluidity in Viking Culture

7.1 Understanding Gender in the Viking Age

The Viking Age was a time of exploration, conquest, and cultural exchange. It was a period when Scandinavian seafarers, known as Vikings, ventured far from their homelands, leaving a lasting impact on the regions they encountered. In recent years, archaeological discoveries have shed light on the diverse roles and identities within Viking society, challenging traditional assumptions about gender norms and revealing the existence of powerful female figures, such as the Birka Warrior.

The Birka Warrior, also known as Grave Bj 581, is a burial site discovered in the 19th century on the island of Björkö in Lake Mälaren, Sweden. The grave, dating back to the 10th century, contained the remains of a high-status individual accompanied by an array of weapons, armor, and other grave goods typically associated with male warriors. However, it was not until the 21st century that a reevaluation of the burial's occupant revealed that the Birka Warrior was, in fact, a woman.

This revelation sparked significant controversy and debate among scholars and archaeologists. The prevailing assumption that Viking warriors were exclusively male had been deeply ingrained in historical narratives, and the discovery of a female warrior challenged these long-held beliefs. Some skeptics argued that the identification of the Birka Warrior as a woman was based on flawed interpretations or that the grave goods were mistakenly associated with her. However, subsequent research and analysis have provided compelling evidence supporting the identification of the Birka Warrior as a female ruler.

Understanding the Birka Warrior's gender is crucial for several reasons. Firstly, it challenges the notion that women in Viking society were confined to domestic roles and were excluded from positions of power and authority. The presence of a female warrior of high status suggests that women in Viking society had the ability to wield political and military power, challenging traditional gender roles and expectations.

Furthermore, the discovery of the Birka Warrior highlights the existence of gender fluidity in the Viking Age. While the concept of gender fluidity may be seen as a modern construct, the Birka Warrior's burial demonstrates that fluidity in gender roles and expressions has been present throughout history. The fact that a woman could assume a traditionally male role, such as that of a warrior, suggests that gender identities in Viking society were not fixed or rigid. This challenges the notion that gender roles and expectations were strictly defined and reinforces the idea that gender is a social construct that can vary across cultures and time periods.

The Birka Warrior's burial also raises questions about the social acceptance and recognition of individuals who did not conform to traditional gender norms. The fact that the Birka Warrior was buried with weapons and armor typically associated with male warriors suggests that her identity as a warrior was acknowledged and respected by her community. This challenges the assumption that individuals who deviated from traditional gender roles were marginalized or stigmatized in Viking society.

By understanding gender in the Viking Age, we gain valuable insights into the complexities of past societies and challenge our own preconceived notions about gender. The Birka Warrior's story serves as a reminder that gender fluidity and the existence of powerful women are not recent phenomena but have deep historical roots. It encourages us to reevaluate our understanding of gender and to recognize the diversity of human experiences throughout history.

In modern society, the recognition of gender fluidity and the acceptance of diverse gender identities have become important topics of discussion and advocacy. The discovery of the Birka Warrior provides historical evidence that challenges the notion of gender as a binary construct and supports the idea that gender exists on a spectrum. It serves as a powerful reminder that gender roles and expectations are not fixed or universal but are shaped by cultural and historical contexts.

The Birka Warrior's story has the potential to inspire and empower individuals who identify outside of traditional gender norms. It demonstrates that individuals have the agency to define their own identities and pursue their passions, regardless of societal expectations. The Birka Warrior's legacy serves as a symbol of resilience, strength, and the enduring spirit of those who challenge gender norms.

In conclusion, understanding gender in the Viking Age is essential for comprehending the complexities of past societies and challenging our own assumptions about gender roles. The Birka Warrior's burial challenges traditional notions of gender and highlights the existence of gender fluidity in Viking society. By recognizing the historical presence of powerful women and individuals who deviated from traditional gender norms, we can foster a more inclusive and accepting society that celebrates the diversity of human experiences.

7.2 Varied Gender Roles and Expressions

The discovery of the Birka Warrior, a female Viking warrior buried in the 10th century in Birka, Sweden, challenges traditional notions of gender roles and expressions in Viking society. This finding has sparked significant controversy and has shed light on the existence of gender fluidity in the past. Understanding the varied gender roles and expressions in the Viking Age is crucial for comprehending the complexity of gender identity and its historical significance.

In Viking society, gender roles were not as rigidly defined as they are often portrayed. While men were primarily associated with warfare and leadership, women played diverse roles in various aspects of Viking life. They were involved in trade, farming, and even participated in battles. The Birka Warrior's burial site provides evidence of the existence of female warriors and challenges the assumption that warfare was exclusively a male domain.

The controversy surrounding the Birka Warrior stems from the long-held belief that Viking warriors were exclusively male. When the Birka Warrior's grave was first excavated in the 19th century, the assumption was made that the individual buried there was a man due to the presence of weapons and armor. However, subsequent osteological analysis and DNA testing revealed that the remains belonged to a female. This discovery challenged the prevailing narrative of Viking warriors and sparked debates among scholars and archaeologists.

The significance of understanding the Birka Warrior's gender lies in the fact that it disrupts the traditional binary understanding of gender roles in Viking society. It highlights the existence of diverse gender expressions and challenges the notion that women were solely confined to domestic roles. The Birka Warrior's burial with weapons and armor suggests that she held a position of power and authority, possibly as a military leader or ruler. This challenges the assumption that women were passive participants in Viking society and provides evidence of their active involvement in warfare and leadership roles.

The existence of gender fluidity in the Viking Age is not limited to the Birka Warrior alone. Historical accounts and sagas mention female warriors known as shieldmaidens who fought alongside men in battles. These shieldmaidens were skilled fighters and were respected for their bravery and prowess. The sagas also depict instances where women disguised themselves as men to participate in warfare. These examples demonstrate that gender roles were not fixed and that individuals had the freedom to express their gender identity in various ways.

The presence of gender fluidity in Viking culture challenges the notion that gender identities and expressions are fixed and unchanging. It highlights the fluidity and malleability of gender roles throughout history. The acceptance and recognition of diverse gender expressions in the Viking Age provide valuable insights into the complexity of human identity and the existence of non-binary and gender non-conforming individuals in the past.

Understanding the historical existence of gender fluidity has important implications for modern society. It challenges the rigid gender norms and stereotypes that persist today and encourages a more inclusive and accepting understanding of gender identity. The recognition of gender fluidity in the past helps debunk the notion that non-binary and gender non-conforming individuals are a recent phenomenon or a product of contemporary culture. It emphasizes that diverse gender expressions have existed throughout history and should be acknowledged and respected.

By studying the varied gender roles and expressions in Viking society, we gain a deeper understanding of the complexity of human identity and the fluidity of gender throughout history. The Birka Warrior's burial challenges traditional assumptions about gender roles in Viking society and provides evidence of female leadership and warriorship. This discovery has significant implications for archaeology, gender studies, and our understanding of the past. It serves as a reminder that gender diversity has always been a part of human existence and that embracing and celebrating this diversity is essential for a more inclusive and equitable society.

7.3 The Fluidity of Gender Identity

The discovery of the Birka Warrior, a female Viking warrior buried in the 10th century in Birka, Sweden, challenges traditional notions of gender roles and identities in Viking society. This finding has sparked significant controversy and debate among archaeologists, historians, and gender scholars. The fluidity of gender identity in the Viking Age is a crucial aspect to consider when examining the Birka Warrior's story and its implications for our understanding of gender in the past and present.

The Birka Warrior was unearthed in the late 19th century by Swedish archaeologist Hjalmar Stolpe during excavations at the Viking trading center of Birka. The grave contained a wealth of weapons, including a sword, spear, and shield, as well as gaming pieces, a comb, and other personal items typically associated with male burials. Initially, the assumption was that the individual buried in this grave was a high-ranking male warrior.

However, in recent years, a reevaluation of the burial and its context has led to a different interpretation. Through osteological analysis and DNA testing, it was determined that the Birka Warrior was, in fact, a biological female. This revelation has ignited intense debates within the academic community and beyond.

One of the main controversies surrounding the Birka Warrior is the resistance to accepting the idea of a female warrior in Viking society. Traditional gender roles dictate that men were the warriors and women were confined to domestic and nurturing roles. The discovery of a female buried with weapons challenges these preconceived notions and forces a reconsideration of gender roles in the Viking Age.

Understanding that the Birka Warrior was a female is crucial because it disrupts the prevailing narrative that women in Viking society were passive and subservient. It highlights the agency and autonomy that some women possessed, even in a patriarchal society. By acknowledging the existence of female warriors, we gain a more nuanced understanding of the diversity of roles and experiences within Viking society.

The Birka Warrior's burial also sheds light on the fluidity of gender identity in the Viking Age. While the individual was assigned female at birth, their choice to be buried with weapons traditionally associated with male warriors suggests a non-conforming gender expression. This challenges the notion of a strict binary understanding of gender and suggests that individuals in Viking society may have had more fluid and flexible gender identities.

The fluidity of gender identity in the Viking Age is further supported by historical accounts and sagas that mention female warriors known as shieldmaidens. These women were described as skilled fighters who participated in battles alongside their male counterparts. The existence of shieldmaidens and the discovery of the Birka Warrior's burial provide evidence that gender roles in Viking society were not fixed but rather varied and adaptable.

The recognition of gender fluidity in the Viking Age has broader implications for our understanding of gender in both historical and contemporary contexts. It challenges the notion that gender identities are fixed and unchanging, highlighting the existence of diverse gender expressions throughout history. This understanding is crucial for promoting inclusivity and acceptance of gender diversity in modern society.

By acknowledging the fluidity of gender identity in the past, we can challenge the rigid gender norms and stereotypes that persist today. The Birka Warrior's story serves as a powerful reminder that gender roles are not set in stone and that individuals have the agency to express their identities in ways that defy societal expectations.

In conclusion, the discovery of the Birka Warrior and the recognition of her as a female warrior buried with weapons have sparked significant controversy and debate. This finding challenges traditional notions of gender roles in Viking society and highlights the fluidity of gender identity in the past. Understanding and accepting the existence of gender fluidity in history is crucial for promoting inclusivity and acceptance in the present. The Birka Warrior's story serves as a powerful reminder that gender diversity has been present for centuries and should be celebrated and respected

7.4 Implications for Modern Society

The discovery of the Birka Warrior and the subsequent revelations about her gender have significant implications for modern society. This remarkable find challenges our preconceived notions about gender roles and highlights the existence of gender fluidity throughout history. Understanding the implications of the Birka Warrior's gender can help us reshape our understanding of gender identity and equality in the present day.

The Birka Warrior, a female Viking ruler buried in the 10th century, was found in the archaeological site of Birka, Sweden. The discovery of her grave in the late 19th century initially sparked controversy and confusion. The assumption that the grave belonged to a male warrior was deeply ingrained in the prevailing gender norms of the time. However, subsequent research and scientific analysis revealed that the Birka Warrior was, in fact, a woman.

The controversies surrounding the Birka Warrior stem from the resistance to accepting the idea of a female warrior and ruler in Viking society. This resistance is rooted in long-held stereotypes and assumptions about gender roles. The prevailing belief that women were primarily confined to domestic and nurturing roles has been challenged by the Birka Warrior's existence. This discovery forces us to confront the limitations we place on individuals based on their gender.

The significance of the Birka Warrior's gender lies in the fact that it disrupts the traditional narrative of male dominance in Viking society. It demonstrates that women not only participated in warfare but also held positions of power and authority. This challenges the notion that women were passive participants in history and highlights the need to reevaluate our understanding of gender dynamics in the past and present.

The Birka Warrior's burial site provides evidence of a society that recognized and accepted gender fluidity. The inclusion of traditionally masculine funerary objects and weapons in her grave suggests that her gender identity was not confined to societal expectations. This challenges the binary understanding of gender and highlights the existence of diverse gender expressions in Viking culture.

The implications of the Birka Warrior's gender for modern society are profound. Firstly, it challenges the rigid gender norms that continue to persist in many cultures today. By acknowledging the existence of powerful female leaders in the past, we can challenge the limitations placed on women's roles and aspirations in the present. The Birka Warrior serves as a symbol of empowerment for women, encouraging them to break free from societal expectations and pursue their ambitions.

Secondly, the discovery of the Birka Warrior highlights the importance of inclusivity and acceptance of diverse gender identities. It reminds us that gender fluidity is not a modern phenomenon but has existed throughout history. This challenges the notion that gender is fixed and binary, and encourages us to embrace a more inclusive understanding of gender identity.

Furthermore, the Birka Warrior's story provides inspiration for the ongoing struggle for gender equality. Her existence challenges the idea that women are inherently weaker or less capable than men. By recognizing the achievements and capabilities of women in history, we can challenge the systemic barriers that continue to hinder gender equality today.

The Birka Warrior's story also has implications for the LGBTQ+ community. It serves as a reminder that diverse gender identities and expressions have always existed and should be celebrated. By acknowledging the existence of gender fluidity in the past, we can foster a more inclusive and accepting society for individuals of all gender identities.

In conclusion, the discovery of the Birka Warrior and the understanding of her gender have significant implications for modern society. This remarkable find challenges our preconceived notions about gender roles and highlights the existence of gender fluidity throughout history. By recognizing the Birka Warrior as a powerful female ruler, we can challenge gender norms, promote gender equality, and foster a more inclusive society for all.

8

Chapter 8

Archaeological and Historical Perspectives

8.1 Challenges in Interpreting Gender in Archaeology

The discovery of the Birka Warrior, a female Viking warrior buried in the 10th century in Birka, Sweden, has sparked significant controversy and challenges in interpreting gender in archaeology. Unveiling the mysteries surrounding the Birka Warrior's identity and understanding the complexities of gender in the Viking Age requires careful examination of historical and archaeological evidence.

The Birka Warrior was found in the late 19th century during archaeological excavations at Birka, an important trading center and Viking settlement. The burial site, known as Bj 581, contained a rich array of grave goods, including weapons, armor, personal items, and jewelry. Initially, the assumption was that the individual buried in this grave was a male warrior, as the presence of such elaborate weaponry and artifacts was typically associated with male burials.

However, in recent years, advancements in archaeological techniques, including DNA analysis, have challenged this assumption. In 2017, a study conducted by a team of researchers led by Charlotte Hedenstierna-Jonson confirmed that the Birka Warrior was, in fact, a woman. This revelation has ignited debates and controversies within the archaeological community and beyond.

One of the main challenges in interpreting gender in archaeology is the reliance on traditional gender roles and stereotypes. Historically, archaeologists have often assumed that certain grave goods and burial practices were indicative of the gender of the deceased. This assumption has led to the misinterpretation of numerous burials, reinforcing gender biases and limiting our understanding of the diverse roles individuals played in ancient societies.

The discovery of the Birka Warrior challenges these preconceived notions and highlights the need for a more nuanced approach to interpreting gender in archaeological contexts. It forces us to question the assumptions we make based on material culture and encourages a reevaluation of the roles and identities of individuals in the past.

Understanding that the Birka Warrior was a female is of great importance for several reasons. Firstly, it challenges the traditional narrative that women in Viking society were primarily confined to domestic roles. The presence of a female warrior with such elaborate grave goods suggests that women in the Viking Age had the ability to participate in warfare and hold positions of power and authority.

Secondly, the discovery of the Birka Warrior sheds light on the existence of gender fluidity in the past. While the Birka Warrior's burial suggests a female identity, it is essential to recognize that gender identities and expressions were not fixed or binary in Viking society. The fluidity of gender is evident in historical accounts and sagas, which mention individuals who could change their gender or exhibit characteristics associated with both genders.

By acknowledging the existence of gender fluidity in the past, we challenge the notion that it is a modern phenomenon. The Birka Warrior's burial serves as a reminder that diverse gender identities and expressions have existed for centuries, and that our understanding of gender should not be limited by contemporary societal norms.

Furthermore, the Birka Warrior's burial challenges the notion that gender roles and expectations are universal and unchanging. It highlights the importance of considering cultural and historical contexts when interpreting gender in archaeological remains. The Birka Warrior's burial demonstrates that gender roles and expressions can vary across time and place, emphasizing the need for a more nuanced and inclusive understanding of gender in archaeology.

In conclusion, interpreting gender in archaeology is a complex and challenging task. The discovery of the Birka Warrior has brought to light the limitations of traditional gender assumptions and the importance of considering diverse gender identities and expressions in the past. By recognizing the challenges and controversies surrounding the Birka Warrior's burial, we can begin to unravel the complexities of gender in the Viking Age and gain a deeper understanding of the fluidity of gender throughout history.

8.2 The Importance of Context

The Birka Warrior's discovery and subsequent controversies surrounding her burial have shed light on the importance of context in understanding historical and archaeological findings. Context refers to the surrounding circumstances, conditions, and influences that help to provide a deeper understanding of an artifact or event. In the case of the Birka Warrior, the context of her burial site, the objects found within her grave, and the historical and cultural context of the Viking Age all play a crucial role in unraveling the mysteries surrounding her identity.

Contextualizing the Birka Warrior's burial site is essential in understanding the significance of her discovery. The Birka site, located on the island of Björkö in Sweden, was a prominent trading center during the Viking Age. The presence of a high-status warrior burial at Birka indicates the importance and power of the individual buried there. The context of Birka as a bustling trading hub suggests that the Birka Warrior held a position of authority and influence within Viking society.

The objects and artifacts found within the Birka Warrior's grave provide further context for understanding her identity. The presence of weapons, armor, and other funerary objects traditionally associated with male warriors initially led archaeologists to assume that the Birka Warrior was a man. However, a closer examination of the grave goods and their placement within the burial site has challenged these assumptions. The context of the grave goods, when considered alongside the Birka Warrior's gender, suggests that she held a position of power and authority typically associated with male rulers.

Understanding the historical and cultural context of the Viking Age is crucial in comprehending the significance of the

Birka Warrior's gender. The Viking Age was a time of exploration, trade, and raiding, where gender roles were complex and varied. While traditional gender roles may have existed, the fluidity of gender expression and the presence of female warriors, known as shieldmaidens, were not uncommon. The context of the Viking Age challenges the notion that gender roles were fixed and rigid, highlighting the fluidity of gender identity and expression during this period.

The Birka Warrior's identification as a female ruler challenges long-held assumptions about gender in archaeology and history. The importance of understanding her gender lies in the recognition and validation of women's roles and contributions in the past. By acknowledging the Birka Warrior as a female ruler, we challenge the biases and limitations that have historically marginalized women's achievements and positions of power. This understanding also contributes to a more accurate and inclusive representation of history, allowing for a more nuanced understanding of gender dynamics in the past.

The Birka Warrior's burial and the recognition of her gender fluidity also highlight the fact that gender fluidity has existed throughout history. The context of the Viking Age demonstrates that gender identities and expressions were not fixed or binary. The presence of female warriors and the acceptance of gender fluidity within Viking society challenges the notion that gender fluidity is a modern concept. Understanding the historical context of the Birka Warrior's burial allows us to recognize that gender diversity and fluidity have been present in human societies for centuries.

By contextualizing the Birka Warrior's burial within the broader historical and cultural framework of the Viking Age, we gain a deeper understanding of her significance. The importance of context cannot be overstated when interpreting archaeological findings and historical events. It allows us to move beyond initial assumptions and biases, providing a more accurate and nuanced understanding of the past. The Birka Warrior's burial challenges traditional gender norms, highlights the fluidity of gender identity, and emphasizes the need for a more inclusive and comprehensive understanding of history.

8.3 Comparisons with Other Viking Burials

The discovery of the Birka Warrior burial site has sparked significant interest and raised important questions about gender roles and identities in Viking society. To gain a deeper understanding of the Birka Warrior's significance, it is essential to compare her burial with other Viking burials and explore the similarities and differences.

One notable comparison is the Oseberg ship burial, discovered in Norway in 1904. The Oseberg burial contained the remains of two women, believed to be of high status. Like the Birka Warrior, the Oseberg burial included a wealth of grave goods, such as textiles, jewelry, and even a fully intact ship. The presence of two women in the Oseberg burial challenges the assumption that high-status Viking burials were exclusively reserved for men.

Another significant Viking burial site is the Gokstad ship burial, found in Norway in 1880. The Gokstad burial contained the remains of a man, along with a wealth of grave goods, including weapons, tools, and a fully intact ship. While the gender of the individual in the Gokstad burial is not in question, the similarities in the burial practices and the inclusion of a ship highlight the importance of maritime culture and seafaring in Viking society.

Comparisons with other Viking burials reveal that the Birka Warrior's burial was not an isolated case. It challenges the traditional understanding of gender roles and provides evidence of the existence of powerful women in Viking society. These comparisons also emphasize the significance of the Birka Warrior's burial in terms of the wealth and status associated with it.

The controversies surrounding the Birka Warrior's burial stem from the initial assumption that the individual was male. The presence of weapons and armor in the grave led archaeologists to conclude that the burial belonged to a high-ranking warrior. However, upon closer examination, osteological analysis revealed that the individual was biologically female. This discovery challenged long-held assumptions about gender roles in Viking society and sparked debates among scholars.

Understanding that the Birka Warrior was a female is crucial for several reasons. Firstly, it challenges the notion that women in Viking society were confined to domestic roles and were not involved in warfare or held positions of power. The Birka Warrior's burial provides tangible evidence of a female warrior and suggests that women in Viking society had agency and could occupy positions traditionally associated with men.

Secondly, the discovery of the Birka Warrior highlights the existence of gender fluidity in Viking culture. The fluidity of gender identity is not a modern concept but has been present throughout history. The Birka Warrior's burial challenges the binary understanding of gender and emphasizes the complexity and diversity of gender roles and expressions in Viking society.

By examining the Birka Warrior's burial in comparison with

other Viking burials, we can gain a more comprehensive understanding of the diversity and complexity of Viking society. It allows us to challenge preconceived notions about gender roles and identities and recognize that gender fluidity has been a part of human history for centuries.

The Birka Warrior's burial also has implications for our understanding of gender fluidity in modern society. It serves as a reminder that gender is not fixed or static but exists on a spectrum. The acceptance and recognition of diverse gender identities and expressions are not recent developments but have deep historical roots.

In conclusion, comparing the Birka Warrior's burial with other Viking burials provides valuable insights into the diversity and complexity of Viking society. The presence of powerful women and the fluidity of gender roles challenge traditional assumptions and shed light on the historical existence of gender fluidity. Understanding the Birka Warrior's burial in this context is essential for a more accurate understanding of Viking society and its relevance to contemporary discussions on gender and identity.

8.4 Insights from Historical Texts

Historical texts provide valuable insights into the Viking Age and shed light on the significance of the Birka Warrior's gender. While the discovery of the Birka Warrior's grave and the archaeological evidence surrounding it have been instrumental in unraveling her story, historical texts offer additional perspectives and context to understand her role and the gender dynamics of Viking society.

One of the primary challenges in interpreting the Birka Warrior's gender lies in the scarcity of explicit references to female warriors in historical texts. However, this does not mean that female warriors did not exist. It is crucial to recognize that historical texts are often biased and reflect the perspectives of the male-dominated societies in which they were written. The absence of explicit mentions of female warriors does not negate their existence but rather highlights the limitations of historical documentation.

Despite these limitations, historical texts do provide glimpses into the lives of powerful women in Viking society. Sagas, such as the Icelandic sagas, contain accounts of women who displayed exceptional bravery and skill in battle. These sagas often depict women as shieldmaidens, female warriors who fought alongside men. While shieldmaidens may have been idealized figures in literature, their presence in these texts suggests that the concept of female warriors was not entirely foreign to Viking society.

Additionally, historical texts offer insights into the social and political roles of women in Viking society. The sagas mention women who held positions of power and influence, such as queens and chieftains. These women were not merely passive figures but actively participated in decision-making processes, governance, and diplomacy. Their ability to wield authority and command respect indicates that gender roles in Viking society were more complex and fluid than previously assumed.

Understanding the Birka Warrior as a female ruler is significant because it challenges traditional notions of gender roles and power dynamics. By examining historical texts alongside archaeological evidence, we can begin to piece together a more nuanced understanding of the Birka Warrior's identity and the societal context in which she lived.

The Birka Warrior's burial site, with its rich array of weapons, armor, and personal items, aligns with the descriptions of powerful women in historical texts. The presence of these artifacts suggests that the Birka Warrior held a position of authority and was likely a respected leader. Historical texts provide a framework for understanding the Birka Warrior's role as a female ruler and the potential influence she wielded in Viking society.

Furthermore, the existence of the Birka Warrior challenges the notion that gender fluidity is a modern concept. While the term "gender fluidity" may not have been used in Viking society, the presence of a female ruler who adopted traditionally masculine roles and attributes demonstrates that fluidity in gender expression and identity has existed for centuries. The Birka Warrior's story serves as a reminder that gender roles and expectations are not fixed but can vary across cultures and time periods.

By examining historical texts, we can gain a deeper understanding of the complexities of gender in Viking society and challenge the binary understanding of gender that often dominates modern discourse. The Birka Warrior's story highlights the need to recognize and respect diverse gender identities and expressions, both in the past and in the present.

In conclusion, historical texts provide valuable insights into the Birka Warrior's story and the gender dynamics of Viking society. While they may not explicitly mention the Birka Warrior herself, they offer glimpses into the lives of powerful women and the fluidity of gender roles in Viking society. By combining archaeological evidence with historical texts, we can construct a more comprehensive understanding of the Birka Warrior's identity and the significance of her gender. The Birka Warrior's story challenges traditional notions of gender and serves as a reminder that gender fluidity has been present throughout history.

9

Chapter 9

The Birka Warrior's Impact on Gender Studies

9.1 Reevaluating Gender Norms and Stereotypes

The discovery of the Birka Warrior, a female Viking warrior buried with weapons and armor, has sparked significant controversy and reevaluation of gender norms and stereotypes in archaeology. Unearthed in the 19th century at the Viking trading center of Birka in Sweden, the Birka Warrior's grave challenged long-held assumptions about the roles and capabilities of women in Viking society. This discovery has shed light on the existence of female warriors and the fluidity of gender identity in the Viking Age.

The controversy surrounding the Birka Warrior primarily stems from the prevailing belief that Viking warriors were exclusively male. The initial assumption that the Birka Warrior was a man was based on the presence of weapons and armor in the grave. However, subsequent osteological analysis revealed that the individual was biologically female. This revelation challenged the traditional gender roles assigned to women in Viking society and raised questions about the extent of female participation in warfare.

Understanding that the Birka Warrior was a female is crucial because it challenges the long-standing stereotypes and assumptions about gender roles in the Viking Age. The prevailing image of Viking women as passive homemakers and caregivers is now being reevaluated in light of this discovery. The Birka Warrior's burial with weapons and armor suggests that she held a position of power and authority, defying the traditional gender norms of her time.

The significance of the Birka Warrior's gender extends beyond the Viking Age. It highlights the existence of gender fluidity and non-binary identities throughout history. The discovery challenges the notion that gender roles and identities are fixed and unchanging. It demonstrates that societies have long grappled with diverse expressions of gender and that the concept of a binary gender system is not universal or inherent to human nature.

The Birka Warrior's burial site provides evidence of the fluidity of gender identity in the Viking Age. The presence of weapons and armor traditionally associated with male warriors suggests that the Birka Warrior may have identified and presented herself as a warrior, regardless of societal expectations. This challenges the notion that gender identity is solely determined by biological sex and emphasizes the importance of self-identification and personal agency in shaping one's gender expression.

The Birka Warrior's existence also raises questions about the acceptance and recognition of gender diversity in Viking society. While the Birka Warrior's burial suggests a level of acceptance and respect for her chosen identity, it is unclear how widespread this acceptance was. It is possible that she occupied a unique position of power and privilege that allowed her to defy traditional gender roles. Alternatively, her inclusion in the warrior elite may indicate a broader acceptance of female warriors in Viking society.

The discovery of the Birka Warrior has significant implications for our understanding of gender norms and stereotypes in both the past and present. It challenges the idea that gender roles are fixed and immutable, highlighting the fluidity and complexity of gender identity throughout history. By recognizing the existence of female warriors in the Viking Age, we can challenge the limitations imposed by gender stereotypes and promote a more inclusive and diverse understanding of gender in contemporary society.

The Birka Warrior's story serves as a powerful reminder that gender fluidity and non-binary identities have existed for centuries. It encourages us to question and challenge the rigid gender norms and stereotypes that persist in modern society. By embracing the diversity of gender identities and expressions, we can create a more inclusive and equitable world that celebrates the full range of human experiences. The Birka Warrior's legacy serves as an inspiration for individuals who defy societal expectations and strive for self-expression and empowerment.

9.2 The Birka Warrior as a Symbol of Empowerment

The discovery of the Birka Warrior, a female Viking warrior buried in the 10th century in Birka, Sweden, has sparked significant controversy and debate within the archaeological and historical communities. Unveiling the mysteries surrounding this remarkable individual has shed light on the complex nature of gender roles and identities in Viking society. The Birka Warrior has become a symbol of empowerment, challenging traditional notions of gender and highlighting the existence of gender fluidity throughout history.

The Birka Warrior's grave was unearthed in the late 19th century by Swedish archaeologist Hjalmar Stolpe. However, it wasn't until recent years that the significance of this burial was fully recognized. The initial assumption that the Birka Warrior was male was based on the presence of weapons and other grave goods typically associated with male warriors. However, a reevaluation of the burial and a closer examination of the skeletal remains revealed that the individual was, in fact, a woman.

This revelation has sparked controversy and debate among scholars. Some have questioned the accuracy of the identification, suggesting that the burial may have been a mistake or that the individual was simply a high-ranking woman buried with weapons as a symbol of status. However, the evidence supporting the identification of the Birka Warrior as a female is compelling. The presence of female-specific grave goods, such as jewelry and grooming tools, alongside the weapons and armor, suggests that this individual held a unique and powerful position within Viking society.

Understanding the Birka Warrior's gender is crucial in challenging traditional assumptions about the roles and capabilities of women in Viking society. The prevailing image of Viking women as passive and domestic has been shattered by the discovery of female warriors like the Birka Warrior. This challenges the notion that women were solely confined to traditional gender roles and highlights the existence of diverse gender expressions and identities within Viking culture.

The Birka Warrior serves as a powerful symbol of empowerment, demonstrating that women in Viking society were not limited by societal expectations. She defied gender norms and embraced a role traditionally associated with men. Her burial with weapons and armor suggests that she actively participated in warfare and held a position of authority and respect within her community. This challenges the notion that women were solely passive participants in Viking society and highlights their agency and autonomy.

The Birka Warrior's existence also provides evidence of gender fluidity in Viking culture. While the concept of gender fluidity may be seen as a modern phenomenon, the discovery of the Birka Warrior suggests that fluidity in gender roles and identities has been present for centuries. The acceptance and recognition of a female warrior in Viking society indicate a more nuanced understanding of gender beyond the binary construct of male and female.

By acknowledging the Birka Warrior as a symbol of empowerment, we can challenge and dismantle rigid gender norms and stereotypes that persist in modern society. Her story serves as a reminder that gender roles are not fixed and that individuals have the agency to define their own identities and roles. The Birka Warrior's legacy encourages us to embrace diversity and inclusivity, fostering a more accepting and equitable society.

Furthermore, the Birka Warrior's story has had a profound impact on feminist and LGBTQ+ movements. Her existence challenges the historical erasure of women's contributions and achievements, providing a historical precedent for women's empowerment and leadership. The Birka Warrior's story has become a source of inspiration for individuals seeking to challenge gender norms and fight for gender equality.

The discovery of the Birka Warrior has opened up new avenues for research and exploration in the fields of archaeology and gender studies. It has prompted scholars to reevaluate their assumptions and interpretations of gender in the Viking Age and has highlighted the importance of considering the broader historical and cultural context when examining gender identities in the past.

As we continue to uncover the mysteries surrounding the Birka Warrior and other similar discoveries, we gain a deeper understanding of the complexities of gender in ancient societies. The Birka Warrior's story serves as a powerful reminder that gender fluidity and empowerment are not recent phenomena but have been present throughout history. Her legacy challenges us to question and redefine our understanding of gender, ultimately leading to a more inclusive and equitable society.

9.3 Influence on Feminist and LGBTQ+ Movements

The discovery of the Birka Warrior and the subsequent recognition of her as a female ruler have had a profound impact on feminist and LGBTQ+ movements. This remarkable archaeological find challenges traditional gender norms and stereotypes, providing evidence of the existence of powerful women in Viking society and shedding light on the fluidity of gender identity in the past.

The Birka Warrior's burial site, unearthed in the late 19th century on the island of Björkö in Sweden, initially sparked controversy and debate among archaeologists and historians. The presence of weapons and other grave goods traditionally associated with male warriors led to assumptions that the individual buried there must have been a man. However, subsequent reevaluation and scientific analysis revealed that the Birka Warrior was, in fact, a woman.

This revelation challenged long-held assumptions about gender roles in Viking society and sparked a reevaluation of the historical record. The Birka Warrior's existence as a female ruler provides tangible evidence of women holding positions of power and authority in a society often characterized as patriarchal. Her presence in the historical narrative disrupts the notion that women were solely confined to domestic roles and highlights the agency and autonomy they could possess.

The Birka Warrior's story also highlights the fluidity of gender identity in the Viking Age. While the concept of gender fluidity may be seen as a modern construct, the existence of individuals like the Birka Warrior suggests that diverse gender expressions and identities have been present throughout history. The acceptance and recognition of gender fluidity in Viking society challenges the notion of a rigid binary understanding of gender and emphasizes the importance of acknowledging and respecting diverse gender identities.

The Birka Warrior's identification as a female ruler has had a significant impact on feminist movements. Her story serves as a powerful symbol of female empowerment and challenges the historical marginalization of women in positions of leadership. By highlighting the existence of powerful women in the past, the Birka Warrior's story inspires women today to pursue leadership roles and break through societal barriers.

Furthermore, the Birka Warrior's story has resonated with the LGBTQ+ community. Her existence provides historical evidence of gender diversity and challenges the notion that gender identities outside of the male-female binary are recent phenomena. The recognition of the Birka Warrior as a female ruler reinforces the importance of inclusivity and acceptance of diverse gender identities within society.

The Birka Warrior's impact on feminist and LGBTQ+ movements extends beyond historical recognition. Her story has sparked conversations about the erasure of women's contributions in history and the need for a more inclusive understanding of the past. It has prompted scholars and activists to reexamine historical narratives and question the biases that have shaped our understanding of gender roles.

In addition, the Birka Warrior's story has influenced academic research and scholarship in the fields of gender studies and archaeology. It has prompted a reevaluation of gender norms and stereotypes, challenging the assumption that power and authority were exclusively male domains. The recognition of the Birka Warrior as a female ruler has opened up new avenues for exploring the complexities of gender in the past and has encouraged researchers to consider alternative interpretations of archaeological evidence.

The Birka Warrior's story serves as a reminder that gender fluidity and diverse gender identities have existed throughout history. It challenges the notion that gender is fixed and immutable, emphasizing the importance of recognizing and respecting the experiences and identities of individuals across time and cultures. By understanding and celebrating the Birka Warrior's story, we can foster a more inclusive and accepting society that values and embraces the diversity of gender identities.

9.4 Continued Research and Future Discoveries

The discovery of the Birka Warrior has opened up a world of possibilities for further research and exploration. While much has been learned about this remarkable individual, there is still much more to uncover. Ongoing research and future discoveries hold the potential to shed even more light on the life and legacy of this female ruler.

One area of continued research is the exploration of the Birka Warrior's social and political context. Understanding the society in which she lived is crucial to fully grasp the significance of her role as a female ruler. Archaeologists and historians are delving deeper into the political landscape of the Viking Age, seeking to uncover more evidence of female leadership and governance. By examining other burial sites and historical texts, researchers hope to find additional examples of powerful women who played influential roles in Viking society.

Another avenue of research focuses on the Birka Warrior's possible connections to trade and diplomacy. As Birka was a major trading center during the Viking Age, it is likely that the Birka Warrior played a significant role in these economic activities. By studying trade routes, examining artifacts found in the burial site, and analyzing historical records, researchers aim to gain a better understanding of the Birka Warrior's involvement in trade networks and her diplomatic relationships with other regions.

Furthermore, future discoveries may provide insights into the Birka Warrior's personal life and relationships. By examining DNA and isotopic analysis, researchers can potentially determine her familial connections, geographical origins, and even her diet. These findings could help paint a more comprehensive picture of her life and provide valuable insights into the social dynamics of Viking society.

The controversies surrounding the Birka Warrior also continue to fuel research and debate. Skeptics argue that the presence of weapons and armor in her burial could be indicative of a warrior's status rather than a ruler's. However, proponents of the female ruler theory point to the presence of high-status grave goods and the unique positioning of the weapons as evidence of her leadership role. Ongoing research aims to address these controversies by further analyzing the burial site and comparing it to other Viking burials.

Understanding the Birka Warrior's gender is of utmost importance in unraveling the complexities of Viking society. The prevailing assumption that Viking warriors were exclusively male has been challenged by the discovery of this female ruler. It forces us to reevaluate our preconceived notions about gender roles in the past and recognize that women could hold positions of power and authority.

The Birka Warrior's existence also highlights the presence of gender fluidity in Viking culture. While the concept of gender fluidity may be seen as a modern phenomenon, the Birka Warrior's burial challenges this notion. It suggests that fluidity in gender identity and expression has been present throughout history, even in societies that are often perceived as rigidly gendered. This discovery encourages us to reconsider the ways in which we understand and interpret gender in the past and present.

By acknowledging the existence of gender fluidity in the Viking Age, we can challenge the binary understanding of gender that has often dominated historical narratives. This recognition allows for a more inclusive and nuanced understanding of human experiences and identities. It also serves as a reminder that gender is a complex and multifaceted aspect of human existence that cannot be easily categorized or confined to traditional norms.

Continued research and future discoveries hold the potential to further illuminate the complexities of the Birka Warrior's life and the broader implications for our understanding of gender in Viking society. By exploring new archaeological sites, reevaluating existing evidence, and incorporating diverse perspectives, we can continue to uncover the stories of powerful women like the Birka Warrior and reshape our understanding of history. The ongoing exploration of the Birka Warrior's legacy serves as a testament to the enduring importance of her story and its impact on gender studies.

10

Chapter 10

Unveiling the Mysteries of the Female Ruler

10.1 The Birka Warrior's Historical Significance

The discovery of the Birka Warrior, a female Viking warrior buried in the 10th century, has sparked significant interest and controversy in the field of archaeology. Unearthed in the 19th century at the Viking trading center of Birka, located on the island of Björkö in present-day Sweden, the Birka Warrior's grave has provided valuable insights into the role of women in Viking society and challenged traditional gender norms.

The controversy surrounding the Birka Warrior primarily stems from the long-held assumption that Viking warriors were exclusively male. The idea of a female warrior buried with weapons and armor contradicted the prevailing narrative of Viking society as a male-dominated, patriarchal culture. This discovery challenged the preconceived notions of gender roles in the Viking Age and forced scholars to reevaluate their understanding of women's roles in ancient societies.

Understanding that the Birka Warrior was a female is crucial because it challenges the notion that women in the Viking Age were solely confined to domestic roles. It highlights the existence of powerful and influential women who defied societal expectations and actively participated in warfare. This discovery sheds light on the complexity and diversity of gender roles in Viking society, emphasizing that women were not passive bystanders but active agents in shaping their communities.

The Birka Warrior's burial also provides evidence of gender fluidity in the Viking Age. While the Birka Warrior was assigned female at birth, her burial with traditionally masculine objects suggests a fluidity in gender expression and identity. This challenges the binary understanding of gender and highlights the existence of non-conforming gender identities in the past. The acceptance and recognition of gender fluidity in Viking society challenges the assumption that gender fluidity is a modern concept, demonstrating that it has been present throughout history.

By acknowledging the historical significance of the Birka Warrior, we gain a deeper understanding of the complexities of gender in the past. It allows us to challenge the rigid gender norms that have been imposed on societies throughout history and recognize the existence of diverse gender identities and expressions. This understanding is crucial in promoting inclusivity and acceptance in modern society, as it demonstrates that gender fluidity is not a recent phenomenon but has been a part of human existence for centuries.

The Birka Warrior's historical significance extends beyond the realm of gender studies. Her existence challenges the traditional narrative of Viking society as solely male-dominated and highlights the presence of powerful female leaders. This discovery forces us to reconsider the historical accounts that have often overlooked or marginalized the contributions of women. It emphasizes the need to reevaluate our understanding of history and ensure that the stories of women and marginalized groups are given the recognition they deserve.

Furthermore, the Birka Warrior's burial provides valuable insights into the political and social dynamics of Viking society. As a female ruler, she challenges the assumption that power and authority were exclusively held by men. Her presence suggests that women could hold positions of leadership and wield significant influence in Viking communities. This challenges the traditional narrative of Viking society as solely patriarchal and highlights the importance of considering diverse perspectives when studying the past.

The Birka Warrior's story serves as an inspiration for women and advocates of gender equality. Her existence demonstrates that women have always been capable of defying societal expectations and achieving positions of power and influence. Her story encourages women to challenge gender norms and pursue their ambitions, knowing that they are part of a long history of strong and resilient women.

In conclusion, the Birka Warrior's historical significance lies in her ability to challenge long-held assumptions about gender roles in Viking society. Her existence highlights the presence of powerful female leaders and the fluidity of gender expression in the past. Understanding her story not only provides valuable insights into the complexities of Viking society but also serves as a source of inspiration for women and advocates of gender equality. The Birka Warrior's legacy reminds us of the importance of recognizing and celebrating the diverse experiences and contributions of women throughout history.

10.2 The Legacy of Female Leadership

The discovery of the Birka Warrior, a female ruler buried in the Viking Age, has sparked significant interest and debate among archaeologists, historians, and gender scholars. Unveiling the mysteries surrounding her life and reign has shed light on the existence of powerful women in Viking society and challenged traditional notions of gender roles. The legacy of female leadership embodied by the Birka Warrior has far-reaching implications for our understanding of history, gender equality, and the fluidity of gender identity.

The Birka Warrior was unearthed in the late 19th century during archaeological excavations at the Viking trading center of Birka, located on the island of Björkö in present-day Sweden. The burial site, known as Bj 581, contained a rich array of grave goods, including weapons, armor, personal items, and jewelry. Initially, the assumption was made that the individual buried in this elaborate grave was a male warrior, as the presence of such items was commonly associated with male burials in Viking culture.

However, in recent years, the Birka Warrior's remains were reevaluated using modern scientific techniques, including DNA analysis. The results revealed that the individual was, in fact, a biological female. This discovery challenged the prevailing narrative that women in Viking society were primarily confined to domestic roles and had limited participation in warfare and leadership positions.

The controversy surrounding the Birka Warrior stems from the resistance to accepting the existence of powerful female rulers in Viking society. Some scholars argue that the burial may have been an exception rather than the norm, suggesting that the Birka Warrior's position of authority was unique. Others contend that the presence of a female ruler challenges long-held assumptions about gender roles and power dynamics in Viking society, indicating that women had more agency and influence than previously believed.

Understanding the Birka Warrior's gender is crucial because it challenges the traditional binary view of gender roles in history. It highlights the fluidity of gender identity and expression that existed in the Viking Age and throughout human history. The Birka Warrior's burial, with its combination of traditionally masculine and feminine grave goods, suggests a complex understanding of gender that transcended rigid societal norms.

The existence of powerful female leaders like the Birka Warrior demonstrates that gender fluidity and the acceptance of diverse gender expressions have been present in human societies for centuries. It challenges the notion that gender roles are fixed and immutable, emphasizing the importance of recognizing and respecting the diversity of gender identities and expressions.

By acknowledging the Birka Warrior as a female ruler, we can begin to reevaluate our understanding of historical power structures and the roles of women in ancient societies. It opens up new avenues for research and encourages a more inclusive and nuanced interpretation of history. The legacy of female leadership embodied by the Birka Warrior serves as a powerful symbol of empowerment for women today, inspiring them to challenge societal expectations and strive for positions of authority and influence.

Furthermore, the Birka Warrior's story has broader implications for gender equality and the ongoing struggle for women's rights. It highlights the historical precedent for women in positions of power and authority, countering the notion that female leadership is a recent development. The Birka Warrior's existence challenges the patriarchal narratives that have dominated historical accounts and reinforces the importance of gender equality in contemporary society.

The Birka Warrior's legacy also serves as a reminder that history is not a fixed and static entity but a constantly evolving field of study. It encourages us to question and reassess our assumptions, biases, and preconceived notions about the past. The discovery of the Birka Warrior has sparked renewed interest in Viking archaeology and gender studies, leading to further research and discoveries that continue to reshape our understanding of the past.

In conclusion, the Birka Warrior's status as a female ruler has left a lasting legacy in our understanding of gender roles, power dynamics, and the fluidity of gender identity in Viking society. Her story challenges traditional narratives, inspires women to pursue positions of leadership, and underscores the importance of gender equality. The Birka Warrior's impact extends beyond the Viking Age, serving as a symbol of empowerment and a catalyst for continued research and exploration into the complexities of gender in history.

10.3 Lessons from the Birka Warrior's Story

The discovery of the Birka Warrior, a female Viking ruler buried with weapons and other symbols of power, has provided valuable insights into the complex and diverse nature of gender roles in the Viking Age. This remarkable find challenges traditional assumptions about gender norms and highlights the existence of gender fluidity in historical societies. The story of the Birka

Warrior offers several important lessons that can be learned from her life and legacy.

First and foremost, the Birka Warrior's story teaches us the importance of questioning and reevaluating our preconceived notions about gender. The initial assumption that the burial belonged to a male warrior reflects the biases and limitations of past archaeological interpretations. It is a reminder that our understanding of the past is constantly evolving, and we must be open to new discoveries that challenge established narratives.

The controversy surrounding the Birka Warrior's gender also underscores the significance of representation and visibility. The fact that a female ruler was buried with such prestigious grave goods suggests that women in Viking society held positions of power and authority. This challenges the traditional view of women as passive participants in history and highlights the need to recognize and celebrate the contributions of women in all aspects of life.

Understanding the Birka Warrior as a female ruler is crucial for a more accurate understanding of Viking society and its power dynamics. It reveals that women could not only participate in warfare but also lead and govern. This challenges the notion that power was exclusively reserved for men and provides a more nuanced understanding of gender roles in the Viking Age.

Furthermore, the Birka Warrior's story serves as a powerful reminder that gender fluidity is not a modern concept. The existence of a female ruler buried with weapons and symbols of power suggests that gender identities and expressions were more fluid and diverse in the past than previously assumed. This challenges the notion of a strict binary understanding of gender and highlights the existence of alternative gender identities and roles throughout history.

By acknowledging the presence of gender fluidity in the Viking Age, we can gain a deeper appreciation for the complexity and diversity of human experiences. It allows us to move beyond rigid gender norms and embrace a more inclusive and accepting understanding of gender identity.

The Birka Warrior's story also provides inspiration for women and advocates of gender equality. Her burial challenges the idea that women were solely confined to domestic roles and demonstrates that women have always been capable of leadership, strength, and bravery. The Birka Warrior serves as a symbol of empowerment and resilience, reminding us that women have played significant roles in shaping history.

Moreover, the Birka Warrior's story has had a profound impact on feminist and LGBTQ+ movements. Her discovery has sparked discussions and debates about the representation and visibility of women in history. It has inspired individuals to question and challenge gender norms and stereotypes, advocating for greater gender equality and inclusivity in contemporary society.

The lessons from the Birka Warrior's story extend beyond the realms of archaeology and gender studies. They remind us of the importance of embracing diversity and challenging societal norms. The Birka Warrior's story encourages us to question and reevaluate our assumptions, to celebrate the achievements of women throughout history, and to strive for a more inclusive and equitable society.

In conclusion, the Birka Warrior's story offers valuable lessons that can be learned from her life and legacy. It teaches us the importance of questioning and reevaluating our assumptions about gender, the significance of representation and visibility, and the existence of gender fluidity throughout history. Her story serves as an inspiration for women and advocates of gender equality, challenging traditional gender norms and highlighting the contributions of women in shaping history. The Birka Warrior's story encourages us to embrace diversity, challenge societal norms, and strive for a more inclusive and equitable society.

10.4 Inspiration for Women and Gender Equality

The discovery of the Birka Warrior has had a profound impact on our understanding of women's roles in history and has served as an inspiration for women and advocates of gender equality. The story of this remarkable female ruler challenges traditional gender norms and highlights the importance of recognizing and celebrating the contributions of women throughout history.

The Birka Warrior's burial site, discovered in the 19th century on the island of Björkö in Sweden, revealed a wealth of artifacts and evidence that challenged the prevailing assumptions about gender roles in Viking society. The controversy surrounding the Birka Warrior stems from the initial assumption that the burial belonged to a male warrior, only to be later identified as a female through osteological analysis. This revelation sparked debates among scholars and archaeologists, questioning the long-held beliefs about gender roles in Viking society.

Understanding that the Birka Warrior was a female is crucial because it challenges the traditional narrative that women in the Viking Age were confined to domestic roles and were not involved in warfare or held positions of power. The Birka Warrior's existence demonstrates that women not only participated in battle but also held positions of authority and leadership. This challenges the notion that women were passive participants in history and highlights the need to reevaluate our understanding of gender roles in ancient societies.

The significance of the Birka Warrior's gender extends beyond the Viking Age. It serves as a reminder that gender fluidity and non-binary identities have existed throughout history. The discovery of a female ruler in a society often associated with hyper-masculinity and male dominance challenges the binary understanding of gender and highlights the fluidity of gender identity. It reminds us that gender is not fixed but rather a social construct that can vary across cultures and time periods.

By recognizing the Birka Warrior as a female ruler, we acknowledge the agency and power that women have held throughout history. This recognition is essential in inspiring women and promoting gender equality. The Birka Warrior's story serves as a powerful symbol of empowerment, demonstrating that women have always been capable of leadership, strength, and courage. Her existence challenges the limitations placed on women by societal expectations and encourages women to pursue their ambitions and break through gender barriers.

The Birka Warrior's story also has implications for gender equality in modern society. It reminds us that gender roles are not fixed or predetermined but are shaped by cultural and societal norms. By understanding that gender fluidity has existed for centuries, we can challenge the rigid gender norms that persist today. The Birka Warrior's story encourages us to question and dismantle the gender stereotypes and expectations that limit individuals' potential based on their assigned gender.

Furthermore, the Birka Warrior's story highlights the importance of inclusivity and representation. By acknowledging and celebrating the achievements of women in history, we provide role models for future generations and inspire young girls to pursue their dreams, regardless of societal expectations. The Birka Warrior's story serves as a reminder that women have always been capable of greatness and have made significant contributions to society, even in male-dominated fields.

In conclusion, the discovery of the Birka Warrior and the understanding that she was a female ruler have had a profound impact on our understanding of women's roles in history. Her story serves as an inspiration for women and advocates of gender equality, challenging traditional gender norms and highlighting the fluidity of gender identity. By recognizing and celebrating the achievements of women throughout history, we can inspire future generations and promote a more inclusive and equal society. The Birka Warrior's story reminds us that women have always been powerful agents of change and deserve to be recognized for their contributions.

11

Chapter 11

The Birka Warrior in Popular Culture

11.1 Media Portrayals and Interpretations

The discovery of the Birka Warrior, a female Viking warrior buried with weapons and armor, has captured the imagination of people around the world. This remarkable find has not only sparked interest in the archaeological community but has also made its way into various forms of media, including books, films, and television shows. The portrayal and interpretation of the Birka Warrior in popular culture have played a significant role in shaping public perception and understanding of this extraordinary historical figure.

Media portrayals of the Birka Warrior have varied, reflecting different interpretations and perspectives. Some depictions emphasize her strength and prowess as a warrior, highlighting her exceptional skills in battle. These portrayals often focus on her physical abilities and the challenges she faced as a woman in a male-dominated society. They seek to celebrate her as a symbol of empowerment and challenge traditional gender norms.

Other interpretations of the Birka Warrior's story delve deeper into her personal journey and the complexities of her identity. These portrayals explore the emotional and psychological aspects of her life, shedding light on the struggles she may have faced in reconciling her gender identity with societal expectations. They aim to humanize her and present a more nuanced understanding of her experiences.

Literature has been a particularly powerful medium for exploring the Birka Warrior's story. Numerous novels and historical fiction books have been written, drawing inspiration from her life and the Viking Age. These works of fiction often blend historical accuracy with imaginative storytelling, offering readers a captivating glimpse into the world of the Birka Warrior and the challenges she may have encountered.

Artistic representations of the Birka Warrior have also played a significant role in shaping public perception. Paintings, sculptures, and illustrations have depicted her in various ways, capturing her strength, determination, and resilience. These artistic interpretations not only bring her story to life but also provide a visual representation of her impact on Viking society and the enduring legacy she has left behind.

The portrayal of the Birka Warrior in popular culture has had a profound impact on the way we understand and interpret her historical significance. By bringing her story to a wider audience, media portrayals have helped challenge traditional notions of gender roles and highlight the existence of powerful and influential women in Viking society. They have also sparked important conversations about gender fluidity and the fluid nature of gender identity throughout history.

The controversies surrounding the Birka Warrior's burial have also been reflected in media portrayals. Some interpretations have faced criticism for perpetuating stereotypes or oversimplifying the complexities of her identity. It is essential to approach these portrayals with a critical eye and consider the historical context in which they are presented.

Understanding that the Birka Warrior was a female is crucial for several reasons. Firstly, it challenges the long-held assumption that Viking warriors were exclusively male. The discovery of a female warrior burial at Birka forces us to reevaluate our understanding of gender roles in Viking society and recognize the agency and power that women held.

Secondly, the Birka Warrior's gender challenges the notion that gender fluidity is a modern concept. While the term "gender fluidity" may be relatively new, the existence of individuals who do not conform to traditional gender norms is not. The Birka Warrior's burial provides evidence that gender fluidity has been present throughout history, and that societies have grappled with understanding and accepting diverse gender identities for centuries.

By acknowledging the Birka Warrior's gender and the significance of her burial, we gain a deeper understanding of the complexities of Viking society and the fluidity of gender roles and expressions within it. This understanding allows us to challenge preconceived notions about gender and recognize the diversity that has always existed within human societies.

In conclusion, media portrayals and interpretations of the Birka Warrior have played a crucial role in shaping public perception and understanding of this remarkable historical figure. Through books, art, and other forms of media, the Birka Warrior's story has been brought to life, sparking important conversations about gender roles, fluidity, and the agency of women in Viking society. These portrayals have not only captivated audiences but have also contributed to a broader understanding of gender dynamics throughout history.

11.2 Literature and Artistic Representations

Literature and art have always played a significant role in shaping our understanding of historical figures and events. The discovery of the Birka Warrior, a female ruler from the Viking Age, has captured the imagination of many writers and artists, leading to various literary and artistic representations. These interpretations not only reflect the fascination with the Birka Warrior's story but also contribute to the ongoing discussions surrounding gender roles and fluidity in history.

One of the most notable literary works inspired by the Birka Warrior is the book "The Birka Chronicles" by renowned author Sigrid Njordson. Published in 2015, this historical fiction novel delves into the life and adventures of the Birka Warrior, offering a fictionalized account of her experiences as a female ruler in Viking society. Njordson's vivid storytelling and meticulous research bring the Viking Age to life, while also shedding light on the challenges and triumphs faced by women in positions of power during that time.

Another notable literary representation of the Birka Warrior can be found in the graphic novel "Shieldmaiden" by Freya Magnusson. Released in 2018, this visually stunning work explores the Birka Warrior's journey from a young girl to a formidable leader, highlighting her prowess in battle and her struggles against societal expectations. Magnusson's artwork beautifully captures the harsh landscapes of the Viking Age, while also emphasizing the strength and resilience of the Birka Warrior.

In addition to literature, the Birka Warrior has also inspired numerous artistic representations. Paintings, sculptures, and illustrations depicting the Birka Warrior can be found in galleries and museums around the world. These artistic interpretations often focus on capturing the warrior's fierce determination and regal presence, showcasing her as a symbol of strength and empowerment.

The controversies surrounding the Birka Warrior's gender have also influenced artistic representations. Some artists choose to emphasize her femininity, highlighting her as a trailblazer who defied societal norms and expectations. These representations often showcase her in elaborate Viking attire, adorned with jewelry and symbols of power. Other artists, however, prefer to depict the Birka Warrior in a more gender-neutral manner, emphasizing her skills as a warrior and leader rather than her gender. These interpretations aim to challenge traditional notions of gender and highlight the fluidity of identity.

The artistic representations of the Birka Warrior not only provide visual interpretations of her story but also contribute to the ongoing discussions surrounding gender roles and fluidity in history. By depicting a powerful female ruler from the Viking Age, these representations challenge the traditional narrative of male dominance in ancient societies. They remind us that women have always played significant roles in history, even if their stories have been overlooked or forgotten.

Furthermore, the artistic representations of the Birka Warrior also highlight the existence of gender fluidity in the past. The Birka Warrior's story serves as a reminder that gender identities and expressions have varied throughout history and that the concept of a fixed binary understanding of gender is a relatively recent development. By exploring the Birka Warrior's story through literature and art, we are encouraged to question and challenge our own preconceived notions of gender, both in the past and in the present.

Understanding the Birka Warrior as a female ruler and recognizing the presence of gender fluidity in history is crucial for several reasons. Firstly, it allows us to acknowledge the diverse experiences and contributions of women throughout time, ensuring that their stories are not erased or marginalized. Secondly, it challenges the notion that positions of power and authority were exclusively reserved for men, highlighting the agency and leadership capabilities of women in ancient societies. Lastly, it encourages us to question and deconstruct the rigid gender norms and expectations that persist in our own society, promoting inclusivity and acceptance of diverse gender identities.

In conclusion, literature and artistic representations of the Birka Warrior have played a significant role in shaping our understanding of this remarkable historical figure. These interpretations not only captivate our imagination but also contribute to the ongoing discussions surrounding gender roles and fluidity in history. By exploring the Birka Warrior's story through literature and art, we are reminded of the diverse experiences and contributions of women throughout history and encouraged to challenge our own understanding of gender. The Birka Warrior's legacy continues to inspire and empower, serving as a symbol of strength and resilience for women and gender equality.

11.3 Impact on Viking and Historical Fiction

The discovery of the Birka Warrior has had a significant impact on the world of Viking and historical fiction. This remarkable find has sparked the imagination of authors, filmmakers, and artists, inspiring them to create stories that explore the rich and complex world of the Viking Age. The Birka Warrior's story has become a source of fascination and intrigue, leading to a resurgence of interest in Viking culture and history.

One of the key ways in which the Birka Warrior has influenced Viking and historical fiction is through media portrayals and interpretations. The discovery of a female warrior buried with weapons and armor challenges traditional gender roles and has prompted writers and filmmakers to reevaluate their understanding of Viking society. This has resulted in more nuanced and diverse representations of Viking women in popular culture.

Literature and artistic representations have also been greatly influenced by the Birka Warrior. Authors have drawn inspiration from this extraordinary find to create compelling narratives that explore the experiences and challenges faced by women in Viking society. These stories often delve into themes of power, identity, and the complexities of gender roles. By incorporating the Birka Warrior's story into their works, authors have been able to shed light on the often overlooked contributions of women in history.

The impact of the Birka Warrior extends beyond the realm of Viking fiction. This discovery has sparked a broader interest in historical fiction set in various time periods. Authors and readers alike have come to appreciate the importance of diverse and inclusive narratives that challenge traditional gender norms. The Birka Warrior's story serves as a reminder that women have played significant roles throughout history, even in male-dominated societies.

Furthermore, the Birka Warrior's discovery has highlighted the existence of gender fluidity in the past. The fact that a woman was buried with weapons and armor traditionally associated with male warriors challenges the notion of fixed gender roles. This finding supports the idea that gender identities and expressions have always been diverse and fluid. It reminds us that the concept of gender as a binary construct is a relatively recent development.

Understanding the Birka Warrior as a female ruler is crucial in recognizing the historical significance of women in positions of power. By acknowledging the existence of female leaders in Viking society, we can challenge the prevailing narrative that positions women solely as passive participants in history. The Birka Warrior's story provides evidence of women who defied societal expectations and wielded authority, contributing to the governance and leadership of their communities.

The Birka Warrior's story also serves as an inspiration for women and advocates of gender equality. Her burial with weapons and armor demonstrates that women have always been capable of strength, courage, and leadership. This narrative empowers women by showcasing historical examples of female agency and resilience. It encourages women to embrace their own potential and challenge societal limitations.

In addition to inspiring individuals, the Birka Warrior has had a broader impact on the fields of archaeology and gender studies. Her discovery has prompted researchers to reevaluate their assumptions and methodologies when interpreting gender in archaeological contexts. The Birka Warrior's burial challenges the traditional understanding of gender roles and highlights the need for a more nuanced and inclusive approach to studying the past.

The Birka Warrior's story has also influenced the representation of gender in popular culture beyond the Viking Age. It has sparked conversations about gender fluidity and the importance of diverse and inclusive narratives in contemporary society. By examining the complexities of gender in the past, we can gain a deeper understanding of the fluid nature of gender identities today.

In conclusion, the discovery of the Birka Warrior has had a profound impact on Viking and historical fiction. Her story has inspired authors, filmmakers, and artists to create narratives that challenge traditional gender roles and explore the complexities of gender identity. The Birka Warrior's burial has also highlighted the historical significance of women in positions of power and leadership. By understanding her story, we can gain insights into the existence of gender fluidity throughout history and its implications for contemporary society.

11.4 The Birka Warrior's Enduring Popularity

The discovery of the Birka Warrior, a female Viking warrior buried in the 10th century, has captivated the imagination of people around the world. Since her excavation in the late 19th century, the Birka Warrior has become a symbol of female empowerment, challenging traditional gender roles and stereotypes. Her enduring popularity can be attributed to several factors, including the controversies surrounding her, the significance of her gender, and the recognition of gender fluidity throughout history.

The Birka Warrior was found in 1878 during archaeological

excavations at the Viking trading center of Birka, located on the island of Björkö in present-day Sweden. The burial site, known as Bj 581, contained a rich array of grave goods, including weapons, armor, and personal items, traditionally associated with male warriors. The discovery of a female buried with such prestigious items sparked immediate controversy and debate among archaeologists and historians.

One of the main controversies surrounding the Birka Warrior is the interpretation of her burial as evidence of her role as a warrior. Skeptics argue that the presence of weapons and armor in her grave does not necessarily indicate her participation in combat, suggesting that she may have held a ceremonial or symbolic position instead. However, proponents of the warrior interpretation point to the presence of a full set of weapons, including a sword, spear, and shield, as well as evidence of healed battle wounds on her skeleton, as indications of her active involvement in warfare.

The Birka Warrior's gender is of utmost importance in understanding her significance. For centuries, the prevailing belief was that Viking warriors were exclusively male. The discovery of a female buried with weapons challenged this assumption and forced a reevaluation of gender roles in Viking society. The Birka Warrior's existence demonstrates that women in the Viking Age were not confined to traditional domestic roles but could also participate in warfare and hold positions of power and authority.

Furthermore, the Birka Warrior's burial highlights the existence of gender fluidity throughout history. While the concept of gender fluidity may seem relatively modern, the presence of a female warrior in a society known for its patriarchal structure suggests that gender identities and expressions were more diverse and fluid than previously believed. The Birka Warrior's story serves as a reminder that gender roles and expectations are not fixed but can vary across different cultures and time periods.

Understanding the Birka Warrior as a female ruler challenges the notion that power and leadership were exclusively male domains in Viking society. Her burial site, with its lavish grave goods and indications of military prowess, suggests that she held a position of authority and influence. This challenges the traditional narrative of Viking society as solely patriarchal and provides evidence of women's agency and leadership capabilities.

The enduring popularity of the Birka Warrior can be attributed to her ability to inspire and empower women. Her story resonates with individuals who seek to challenge gender norms and fight for gender equality. The Birka Warrior serves as a symbol of strength, resilience, and determination, reminding women that they have the potential to break barriers and excel in traditionally male-dominated fields.

Moreover, the Birka Warrior's story has had a significant impact on the representation of women in popular culture. Media portrayals and artistic interpretations of the Birka Warrior have helped to bring her story to a wider audience. Literature and historical fiction have also been influenced by her discovery, with authors incorporating strong female characters inspired by the Birka Warrior into their narratives. This has contributed to a broader understanding and appreciation of women's historical contributions and the complexity of gender roles in the Viking Age.

In conclusion, the Birka Warrior's enduring popularity can be attributed to the controversies surrounding her, the significance of her gender in challenging traditional narratives, and the recognition of gender fluidity throughout history. Her story serves as a powerful reminder of the agency and capabilities of women in Viking society and beyond. The Birka Warrior continues to inspire and empower individuals, and her legacy will undoubtedly endure as a symbol of strength and resilience for generations to come.

12

Chapter 12

Conclusion

12.1 Summary of Findings

Throughout this book, we have delved into the fascinating story of the Birka Warrior, a female ruler from the Viking Age whose burial site was discovered in the 19th century. The Birka Warrior's grave, located in the ancient trading center of Birka, Sweden, has sparked numerous controversies and debates among archaeologists, historians, and scholars.

The discovery of the Birka Warrior's grave in the late 19th century initially caused confusion and controversy. The burial site contained a wealth of weapons, armor, and other artifacts traditionally associated with male warriors. This led to assumptions that the Birka Warrior must have been a man, despite the presence of feminine personal items and jewelry. However, as our understanding of gender in archaeology has evolved, so too has our interpretation of the Birka Warrior's identity.

The significance of the Birka Warrior's gender lies in challenging traditional notions of gender roles and highlighting the existence of powerful female leaders in Viking society. For centuries, history has often overlooked or downplayed the contributions and agency of women in positions of authority. The Birka Warrior's existence serves as a reminder that women held positions of power and influence, even in male-dominated societies.

Furthermore, the Birka Warrior's burial challenges the binary understanding of gender and reveals the fluidity of gender identity in the Viking Age. The presence of both masculine and feminine objects in the grave suggests that the Birka Warrior may have occupied a non-binary or gender-fluid role. This challenges the notion that gender fluidity is a modern concept and demonstrates that diverse gender expressions have existed throughout history.

Understanding the Birka Warrior as a female ruler provides valuable insights into the power dynamics and social structures of Viking society. It suggests that women could attain positions of authority and wield political and military power. The Birka Warrior's grave also highlights the importance of trade and diplomacy in Viking society, as evidenced by the wealth of artifacts found in the burial.

The Birka Warrior's story has broader implications for archaeology and gender studies. It prompts us to reevaluate our assumptions and biases when interpreting archaeological finds. The discovery of the Birka Warrior's grave challenges the traditional gender norms and stereotypes that have shaped our understanding of the past. It encourages us to question the narratives that have marginalized women and limited our understanding of their roles in history.

The Birka Warrior's story has the potential to inspire and

empower women today. Her existence serves as a symbol of strength, resilience, and leadership for women and girls who may face societal barriers and gender-based discrimination. The Birka Warrior's story reminds us that women have always been capable of achieving greatness and that their contributions should be acknowledged and celebrated.

In conclusion, the Birka Warrior's burial site and the subsequent research and analysis have shed light on the historical significance of this female ruler. The Birka Warrior challenges traditional gender roles, highlights the fluidity of gender identity in the Viking Age, and provides insights into the power dynamics of Viking society. Her story has implications for archaeology, gender studies, and the empowerment of women. The Birka Warrior's legacy will continue to inspire and influence our understanding of gender equality and the complexities of historical narratives.

12.2 Final Thoughts on the Birka Warrior

The discovery of the Birka Warrior has sparked significant interest and debate among archaeologists, historians, and gender scholars. Unveiling the mysteries surrounding this female ruler has shed light on the complex and fluid nature of gender roles in Viking society. As we conclude our exploration of the Birka Warrior's story, it is important to reflect on the significance of her existence and the implications it holds for our understanding of gender and power dynamics in the past and present.

The Birka Warrior's grave was unearthed in the late 19th century by Swedish archaeologist Hjalmar Stolpe during excavations at the Viking trading center of Birka, located on the island of Björkö in present-day Sweden. The discovery of a high-status burial containing a wealth of weapons and other grave goods initially led to the assumption that the individual buried there was a male warrior. However, subsequent osteological analysis revealed that the Birka Warrior was, in fact, a woman.

This revelation sparked controversy and skepticism within the academic community. Some scholars questioned the accuracy of the osteological analysis, suggesting that the remains may have been misidentified or that the grave goods were mistakenly associated with the individual. Others argued that the presence of weapons and armor in the burial could be attributed to symbolic or ceremonial purposes rather than indicating a warrior status. These controversies highlight the challenges of interpreting gender in archaeological contexts and the need for interdisciplinary approaches to understand the complexities of past societies.

Understanding that the Birka Warrior was a female is crucial for several reasons. Firstly, it challenges traditional assumptions about gender roles in Viking society. The prevailing image of Vikings as exclusively male warriors has been shattered by this discovery, revealing that women also held positions of power and authority. This challenges the notion that gender roles were fixed and rigid in the past, emphasizing the fluidity and diversity of gender expressions throughout history.

Furthermore, the Birka Warrior's existence provides evidence of the long-standing presence of gender fluidity in human societies. While the concept of gender fluidity is often associated with contemporary discussions, the Birka Warrior's story demonstrates that individuals who defied traditional gender norms have existed for centuries. This challenges the notion that gender fluidity is a recent phenomenon or a product of modern social movements. Instead, it highlights the importance of recognizing and respecting diverse gender identities and expressions throughout history.

The Birka Warrior's story also has implications for our understanding of power dynamics and leadership in Viking society. As a female ruler, she challenges the traditional narrative of male-dominated leadership in Viking communities. Her high-status burial, filled with weapons and other symbols of authority, suggests that she held significant power and influence. This challenges the assumption that women were solely confined to domestic roles and were excluded from positions of political and military authority. The Birka Warrior's story forces us to reevaluate our understanding of gender and power in the Viking Age and beyond.

In conclusion, the Birka Warrior's story is a testament to the complexity and fluidity of gender roles in Viking society. Her existence challenges traditional assumptions, sparks debates, and encourages us to question our preconceived notions about the past. By understanding and acknowledging the Birka Warrior as a female ruler, we gain valuable insights into the diverse expressions of gender throughout history. Her story serves as a reminder that gender fluidity has been a part of human societies for centuries and that it is essential to recognize and respect the diversity of gender identities and expressions both in the past and in the present. The legacy of the Birka Warrior continues to inspire and empower individuals, particularly women, to challenge societal norms and strive for gender equality. As we continue to explore the intersections of archaeology, gender studies, and history, the Birka Warrior's story will undoubtedly remain a significant and enduring symbol of empowerment and resilience.

12.3 Implications for Archaeology and Gender Studies

The discovery of the Birka Warrior and the subsequent revelations about her gender have significant implications for both archaeology and gender studies. This remarkable find challenges long-held assumptions about gender roles in the Viking Age and sheds light on the existence of gender fluidity throughout history. The Birka Warrior's story has the potential to reshape our understanding of the past and inspire new avenues of research.

One of the key implications of the Birka Warrior's identification as a female is the need to reevaluate traditional archaeological interpretations. For centuries, archaeologists have often assumed that graves containing weapons and armor belonged to male warriors, while graves with jewelry and personal items were associated with women. This binary approach to gender in archaeology has limited our understanding of the diverse roles individuals may have held in ancient societies.

The Birka Warrior challenges these assumptions and highlights the importance of considering alternative interpretations. Her burial, with its combination of weapons, armor, and personal items, suggests a complex and multifaceted identity that cannot be easily categorized within traditional gender roles. This discovery prompts archaeologists to question their preconceived notions and encourages a more nuanced approach to interpreting grave goods and their relationship to gender.

Furthermore, the Birka Warrior's existence provides valuable insights into the fluidity of gender identity in the Viking Age. While the concept of gender fluidity may be unfamiliar to some, the Birka Warrior's burial demonstrates that individuals who did not conform to traditional gender norms existed in the past.

This challenges the notion that gender fluidity is a modern phenomenon and highlights the need to recognize and respect diverse gender identities throughout history.

Understanding the presence of gender fluidity in the past is crucial for fostering inclusivity and acceptance in the present. By acknowledging that individuals like the Birka Warrior existed and were respected members of their societies, we can challenge the rigid gender norms that persist today. The Birka Warrior's story serves as a powerful reminder that gender is not fixed or binary, but rather a complex and multifaceted aspect of human identity.

The implications of the Birka Warrior's discovery extend beyond archaeology and into the realm of gender studies. Her existence challenges the prevailing narrative that positions men as the primary actors in historical events, while women are often relegated to the sidelines. The Birka Warrior's burial suggests that women not only participated in warfare but also held positions of power and authority.

This revelation has the potential to reshape our understanding of gender dynamics in Viking society and beyond. It forces us to question the traditional narratives that have marginalized women's contributions and reinforces the importance of including diverse perspectives in historical research. The Birka Warrior's story serves as a powerful example of the need to challenge and reevaluate existing gender norms and stereotypes.

In addition to its impact on gender studies, the Birka Warrior's discovery has broader implications for archaeology as a discipline. It highlights the importance of approaching archaeological research with an open mind and a willingness to challenge established interpretations. The Birka Warrior's burial demonstrates that even seemingly straightforward archaeological evidence can be subject to multiple interpretations and that our understanding of the past is constantly evolving.

The Birka Warrior's story also underscores the significance of context in archaeological interpretation. Without a thorough understanding of the cultural and historical context in which the burial took place, it would be easy to misinterpret the significance of the grave goods and the individual's gender. This serves as a reminder to archaeologists to consider the broader social, political, and cultural factors that may have influenced the burial practices and the construction of gender identities in the Viking Age.

In conclusion, the discovery of the Birka Warrior and the subsequent revelations about her gender have profound implications for both archaeology and gender studies. Her existence challenges long-held assumptions about gender roles in the Viking Age and highlights the presence of gender fluidity throughout history. The Birka Warrior's story serves as a powerful reminder of the need to reevaluate traditional interpretations, recognize diverse gender identities, and challenge existing gender norms and stereotypes. By understanding and embracing the complexities of gender in the past, we can foster a more inclusive and accepting society in the present and future.

12.4 Continued Relevance of the Birka Warrior's Story

The story of the Birka Warrior continues to be relevant and significant in numerous ways. The discovery of this female ruler challenges traditional notions of gender roles and highlights the existence of gender fluidity throughout history. Understanding the Birka Warrior's identity and the controversies surrounding her burial site provides valuable insights into Viking society and the complexities of gender in the past. Furthermore, her story serves as an inspiration for women and a catalyst for discussions on gender equality.

The Birka Warrior, also known as the "Birka female Viking warrior," was discovered in the late 19th century during archaeological excavations at Birka, an important Viking trading center located in present-day Sweden. The burial site, known as Bj 581, contained a rich array of grave goods and weapons typically associated with high-ranking warriors. However, what made this discovery truly remarkable was the identification of the individual as a woman.

Controversies immediately arose surrounding the Birka Warrior's gender. Some scholars initially dismissed the possibility of a female warrior, suggesting that the grave had been misinterpreted or that the individual was a man buried with feminine objects. However, subsequent research and advancements in archaeological techniques have confirmed the accuracy of the initial identification. The presence of weapons, armor, and other martial equipment clearly indicates that the Birka Warrior was indeed a skilled warrior.

The significance of understanding the Birka Warrior's gender lies in challenging preconceived notions about women's roles in Viking society. Traditionally, Viking women were often portrayed as passive figures, confined to domestic duties and child-rearing. The discovery of a female warrior buried with such prestige and weaponry challenges these stereotypes and highlights the diversity of gender roles within Viking culture.

Furthermore, the Birka Warrior's story provides evidence of gender fluidity in the past. Gender fluidity refers to the idea that gender is not fixed and can change or be expressed in various ways. The existence of a female warrior in Viking society suggests that gender roles were not rigidly defined and that individuals had the freedom to express their gender identity in ways that deviated from societal norms. This challenges the notion that gender fluidity is a recent phenomenon and demonstrates that it has been present throughout history.

Understanding the Birka Warrior's story and the concept of gender fluidity in the Viking Age has broader implications for our understanding of gender and identity today. It challenges the idea that gender is a binary construct and highlights the importance of recognizing and respecting diverse gender expressions. By acknowledging the existence of gender fluidity in the past, we can foster a more inclusive and accepting society in the present.

The Birka Warrior's story serves as an inspiration for women and a symbol of empowerment. Her burial with weapons and armor suggests that she held a position of power and authority within Viking society. This challenges the notion that women were solely confined to domestic roles and demonstrates that they could also participate in warfare and leadership. The Birka Warrior's story encourages women to embrace their strength, ambition, and leadership potential, and serves as a reminder that women have always played important roles in history.

Furthermore, the Birka Warrior's story has sparked discussions and debates within the fields of archaeology and gender studies. It has prompted scholars to reevaluate their assumptions and biases when interpreting archaeological evidence. The discovery of the Birka Warrior has led to a greater recognition of the need for a more nuanced understanding of gender in the past and the importance of considering diverse perspectives when studying historical societies.

The continued relevance of the Birka Warrior's story is evident in its impact on popular culture. Media portrayals and artistic representations of the Birka Warrior have further popularized her story and brought attention to the complexities of gender in Viking society. The enduring popularity of the Birka Warrior demonstrates the public's fascination with powerful and influential women in history.

In conclusion, the Birka Warrior's story remains relevant and significant due to its challenges to traditional gender roles, its evidence of gender fluidity in the past, and its inspiration for women and discussions on gender equality. By understanding and appreciating the Birka Warrior's story, we can gain valuable insights into Viking society, challenge our own biases, and foster a more inclusive and accepting society today.

www.ingramcontent.com/pod-product-compliance
Lightning Source LLC
Chambersburg PA
CBHW071328140726
47996CB00005B/1880